As Good As I Want To Be

As Good As I Want To Be

A Parent's Guide to Help Your Teen Succeed

Jack R. Christianson

ALTI
PUBLISHING

Acknowledgments

A special thanks to Jack Rose for suggesting this project. To Wayne Hilbig, President of ALTI Publishing, for taking a chance with the manuscript. To Shelby West for her help with typing, and Ron Louw for his computer skills. And to Steve Young for the foreword and his great example to youth of the world.

Library of Congress number 98-071164

Portions of this book were adapted from one of Jack Christianson's previous works, *What's So Bad About Being Good?* (Bookcraft, 1992).

ALTI Publishing

P.O. Box 28025, San Diego, California 92198-0025, USA
E-mail: whilbig@altipublishing.com

Copyediting: Sherri Schottlaender
Cover design: Robert Aulicino/Pro-Art Graphic Design
Interior design: Kathleen Thorne-Thomsen

Printed in the United States of America
10 9 8 7 6 5 4 3 2 1

ISBN 1-883051-19-3
Distributed to the trade by National Book Network (800) 462-6420

For Melanie

Foreword

On one occasion I was being interviewed over national television and the sports announcer's final question was, "Steve, what most do you want to be remembered for?" The question made me stop for a minute for I knew that he was expecting a football related answer, yet as I thought honestly about my response I could only think of one thing. I said, "I want to be remembered for being a good man."

I know that many people will say that the definition of "good" is relative and means different things to different people, yet when it comes right down to what "good" means I believe it crosses generations and cultures in very similar ways. Integrity, honesty, charity, unselfishness, serving, caring, and acknowledging with gratitude is all part of "good." The greatest thing about being "good" is that it is something we can choose. We can make a decision in almost every circumstance that can be considered "good". We can opt not to hurt others. We can choose to obey laws, care for one another and share our time and substance.

I am proud I am an American and yet as I have traveled throughout the world I am amazed at the goodness of people in all of the countries where I have been. I have observed mothers toward their children, sales people, attendants, people who rush to help others in need. It is something basic and it makes a difference in us all. When goodness is sacrificed for personal gain everyone sacrifices and someone suffers. When one good choice is made it effects many others, especially ourselves. It's like the old Chinese proverb:

When there is righteousness in the heart,
There is beauty in the character.
When there is beauty in the character,
There will be harmony in the home.
When there is harmony in the home,
There will be order in the nation.
When there is order in the nation,
There will be peace in the world.

Some time ago I was visiting a family with several children and I overheard a teenager talking about his teacher. It impressed me because he said, "You know what? If my teacher believes these things are right, they must be right for he is such a "cool stud."

Recognizing that for a sixteen year old boy that was the ultimate compliment I became curious as to who was his teacher. The young boy's mother said it was Jack Christianson; a teacher at their local high school. I paid attention at that point and found out that he had through the years taught thousands of teenagers, both in high school and college. He too had played on a football scholarship throughout college and then had many opportunities to continue with football and also numerous invitations to go into business, yet he turned down these lucrative possibilities because he wanted to help young people experience the feelings of choosing that which is good.

I soon had the privilege to meet Jack Christianson and witnessed myself his rapport with his students. They honored and admired him because he honored and admired them. I became aware of the dedication he felt in the service of others. Jack not only taught every day, authored many books for young people, lectured two or three times a week, but has taken troubled children into his home, opening his door during all hours of the day and night to his needy students. He brings them in, holds them, cries with them and helps them formulate a plan that makes a difference in their lives. Jack travels throughout the country to promote the concept that there is nothing wrong with being "good." He encourages parents to "hold on" for the worth of their child is priceless.

One particular exhausting experience I know of sums up the dedicated life of Jack Christianson. One challenging day Jack had dealt with many tragic circumstances, ending up at the hospital in the early hours of the morning with an attempted suicide of a young girl. He came home emotionally drained with just enough time to get ready to go to work by 7:00 a.m. His sweet wife Melanie had witnessed his pace and once again remembered the statement of one of the beloved leaders of their church, which had always been an inspiration to Jack. "My life is like my shoes, to be worn out in service." That afternoon Melanie purchased a much needed pair of shoes and put them on her weary husband's pillow with a note, "another pair of shoes to be worn out in the service of others."

As this book reaches out to the parents and leaders of youth, its concepts are simple and easy, they need only be considered then tried. It is basic to our inner feelings that we can discern that which is good and acting upon these feelings we can be *As Good As I Want To Be.*

Steve Young
Quarterback San Francisco 49'ers

Contents

Nothing is more important for the public wealth than to train youth in wisdom and virtue.

—Benjamin Franklin

Chapter One

The Worth of an Individual

C hristmas Eve 1988 was bitter cold. The thermometer had plunged to zero, and eighteen to twenty-four inches of snow blanketed the ground. It was a day when wise people were inside with the heater turned up, the fire blazing, and a blanket wrapped securely around them.

My family was busy preparing for our customary Christmas Eve activities: meeting in our family room to open one gift apiece, eat great food, and participate in the yearly reenactment of the Christmas story found in the second chapter of Luke in the New Testament.

The house was filled with the savory aromas of cooking turkey and pumpkin pie. I guess—I couldn't smell them. My nose felt stuffy, my head pounded, my entire body ached with the flu. Everyone was having a marvelous time. Everyone but me. Staying in bed, sick, on Christmas Eve is not my idea of fun. However, I knew if I didn't I wouldn't be well enough to enjoy Christmas morning.

I tried to give orders from bed, but no one seemed to pay much attention, especially when I asked my daughters to let our dog, Grizzly, out for a few minutes.

No one moved. They weren't going outside for anyone. My three oldest daughters all had "reasons" why none of them could go. Finally, however, Rebecca (the oldest) let Grizzly out through the front door. But she didn't stay with him, driven inside by the cold.

A couple of hours later I asked if anyone had let the dog out. Silence was all that came up the stairs into my bedroom. Then Rebecca's anxious voice pierced the quiet. "Oh, Dad, I'm sorry! I forgot about the dog!"

I leaped from my bed, dressed quickly, and ran outside. My illness seemed to remain in the bedroom. It was replaced by the fear of losing my prized golden retriever.

Yelling and whistling for the dog proved fruitless. When Grizzly did not respond, it was evident one of two things had happened: either he had been hit by a car or he had been stolen. He had always come when called.

My heart was sick. My wife, Melanie, and I split up to search for him through the biting cold. We met a few minutes later at the corner, both frozen and wanting the warmth and comfort of our home.

While we discussed our next plan of action, a man pulled up in a blue van. "Are you Jack Christianson?" he asked calmly.

"Yes, sir. Who are you?"

He told me his name and continued, with some hesitation, "I'm your paperboy's father. Your dog followed my son home from his paper route and was hit by a truck in front of our home. Would you please come and decide what you want to do with the body?"

"Is he dead?" I asked, with little hope in my voice.

"Not yet," he replied sadly. "But I'm not sure how long he'll stay alive."

We climbed into the van in silence. Quietly we rode to the scene of the accident. Melanie didn't say anything but covered her face with her hands in order to camouflage her tears. It didn't work; the tears dripped off the heels of her hands into her lap.

Our eyes met. Through her eyes, she communicated a heartfelt message. "I'm sorry, Jack. I know how much you love your dog."

When we arrived at the scene of the accident, a crowd of concerned neighbors stood around the dog's broken body, now covered with someone's coat. One of the neighbors brought a blanket as we approached the dog, and the animal-control officer had already arrived with an ambulance. Okay, it wasn't really an ambulance; it was an animal-control department truck with a cage in the back. But I viewed it as the ambulance that would transport Grizzly to the hospital for treatment.

The sound of my voice brought Grizzly's head up off the cement. His body was stretched across the curb, the front half lying on the sidewalk and the hind legs lying helplessly in the gutter. He tried to get up, but his efforts were in vain. Both back legs were shattered. I calmed him by speaking in soft tones and giving love pats on his head and neck. I cried as I checked out his condition.

When I checked his eyes and gums, it was obvious he was quickly going into shock. I asked the officer if there was a veterinarian on call somewhere in the vicinity.

"It's Christmas Eve," he said, somewhat hesitantly. "But I'll try anyway."

While he talked with the dispatcher, an older gentleman, bundled up in a winter parka and a dirty baseball cap, approached us slowly.

"That your dog, son?" he asked, trying to fight back tears.

"Yeah."

"There was nothing I could do! He just darted in front of my truck! I didn't even have time to hit my brakes."

"It's okay," I said. "I'm sure there was nothing you could have done."

"I'm sorry, son. I'm sorry."

I felt as sorry for him as I did for the dog. He walked away, dejected, hands in his pockets, his head down, mumbling through his tears how sorry he was.

3

"I found one!" the officer said. "The vet will meet us at his office in fifteen to twenty minutes. He's at the mall finishing his Christmas shopping, but he said your golden retriever was worth stopping everything else."

"Thanks," I muttered as I picked up my friend Grizzly and walked toward the "ambulance."

The man who had brought us to the scene of the accident gave my wife a ride home while the officer and I transported my dog to the "hospital."

Melanie arrived at the veterinarian's office shortly after I had carried Grizzly in and placed him on a long, coal-black table. As she watched the doctor and me work on Grizzly, she covered her face with her hands, again trying to hide her tears. It didn't work. Again they found their way to the heels of her hands and then onto the black-and-white checkered tile floor. She was as heartbroken for me as she was for the dog.

Approximately two-and-a-half hours later the doctor gave me the bad news.

"I'm sorry, Jack. I've done all I can do, short of surgery, and I don't think Griz will live through that. It would cost a few hundred dollars, and he'd never make it," he said sadly. "My suggestion is that we put him to sleep. Would you like some time to think about it and to talk it over with your wife?" he asked sympathetically.

"Sure. Thanks," I said, trying now to fight back my tears.

Melanie and I decided it would be best to let Grizzly's suffering end. So, after a few minutes alone with my faithful friend, I kissed him good-bye, asked him to forgive me, and then asked the doctor to do his part quickly.

Within ten seconds after the doctor injected a drug into Grizzly's right front leg, the dog's eyes rolled upward and he was dead. I cried.

Later, while making arrangements for Grizzly's burial, I asked the doctor what he did with the bodies of deceased animals. He said he usually sent them to California. A truck would come for pickup on the following Tuesday, and the weather was cold enough so that Grizzly's body would stay frozen until then. I asked what happened when the bodies reached California. I was sickened at the response.

"Oh, they make fertilizer or glue out of them," he said, without batting an eye.

I thought about all the white paste or glue I had eaten out of those big white jars in elementary school. My stomach turned at the thought.

I instantly determined that my favorite dog was not going to be used as paste in some elementary school somewhere, ending up on the back side of a picture of Abraham Lincoln or George Washington. I made arrangements to take Grizzly and bury him myself.

How would I tell the children that our dear friend was gone? They would be heartbroken. When I told them, they asked if they could kiss him good-bye before we laid him to rest. I know some people might think it morbid for sweet young girls to kiss a dead, stiff dog, but he was part of our family.

My father arrived later to help with the burial. We put chains on my car tires and drove to the foothills of a large mountain overlooking our little valley. Dad only recently returned after being out of the country for a little over a year, so we had much to talk about as we fought the frozen ground and rocky soil to dig the grave.

For some strange reason, as I continued to pick away at the earth, thoughts of pioneer mothers leaving their dead children in shallow graves all along the westward trail flashed through my mind. I was only burying a dog. How would it feel to lay a child or spouse to rest under a thin blanket of snow, or wrapped in a quilt and placed under a bush? Tears found their way off the end of my nose or to the back of my hand as I tried to hide them from my dad. Feelings were deep. A new and deeper appreciation for ancestors was being born. How did they endure?

With these thoughts burning in my mind, I helped lift a large rock in place as a headstone. We had finished our painful task. We rested, leaning on the handles of our shovel and pick. The sun's long white rays filtered through some evening clouds and rested upon us. It was beautiful and peaceful, but bitter cold.

The silence was broken when I asked my dad a question, and the ensuing conversation proved to have a profound influence in my life.

"Can you believe I feel this way over a silly dog?"

"No!" he said quickly, "You've lost countless dogs and other animals, son. Why would this one be so different?"

I don't remember answering specifically, but I do remember asking him another question. Little thought went into it at that moment, but it began a process of profound thought and led to a rich, religious experience between a father and his grown son.

"Dad, if you and I as mortals can weep at the loss of a dog, how must God feel when he loses one of his children or sees people suffer?"

"What?" he asked

"Think about it. If we, as mortals, with all of our frailties and imperfections, can weep when we lose a pet, cannot God, the Almighty, the perfect one, weep when his children choose to abandon him or treat each other poorly?" There on the hillside overlooking the valley where my dad had raised me, a father and son had a deep religious experience discussing the worth of souls and the value of people in the sight of God. It was too cold to talk for long, but seeds were planted deeply, not to be forgotten with the melting snow.

With all my heart I believe that every human being is of great worth and value. I'm not saying that they are just good, or okay, or fine, but great! Of course, we are of far more value to God and to each other than my dog was to me.

We mortals cry over the loss of animals and physical possessions. Why, then, do we not cry more over each other? Why are we so intolerant of each other? Why are we so cruel? Why when we see each other pursuing lifestyles that are self-destructive or destructive of others do we have the attitude "It's their life and they can destroy it if they want to?" We do all we can to provide our animals with the most comfortable life possible. What about people?

I remember when our daughter's hamsters, Josey and Marilyn died. It was a sad occasion at the Christianson home—except for me. To me they were just rodents that ran all night, every night, in a squeaking metal wheel. When I removed the wheel, they decided to climb the water bottle and bang it against the glass all night. They drove me crazy! But to our daughter Molly they were beloved pets. Josey died first and not much was said. Then Marilyn died. Tears trickled down an eight-year-old's face as the cage was cleaned out for the last time and the pet who had become a dear friend was placed in a shoe box and buried in the backyard.

Then there was a similar occasion. While I cleaned another daughter's fish tank, two small fish flipped out of my net and went down the drain in the bathroom sink. You would have thought I had committed murder! My daughter Rebecca cried over fish.

Can't we cry over each other and over one another's sufferings? Can't we just say hello when we pass on the street? Can't we lift one another rather than always putting one another down? What kind of world would this be if we just cared for people as much as we care for animals? Oh, I'm aware that some readers may think me to be a guardian of morality or to be too preachy; however, someone has to say it. Human beings are of great worth! We must believe it! When we do, the entire world can be changed. I'm also aware that some readers may consider themselves to only be advanced animals and not of divine origin. You certainly are free to believe that if you wish, but I do not. I believe that every person of every religion, race, country, or creed is important. We all have value and deserve to be treated with dignity. Jesus taught that the greatest way to show your love was to be willing to lay down your life for a friend (see John 15 of the New Testament). You and I will probably not be required to lay down our lives for anyone. But can we not be kind and considerate? Can we not lift and build rather than destroy and degrade?

Two or three days after Grizzly's death I tried to find another puppy to take his place. I contacted the people we had bought him from, and they offered to give us his mother if we would breed her with a particular male and then give them a puppy. After looking at the mother dog, Ginger, I decided to do it. She was the same color as Grizzly, but two or three inches shorter at the shoulder, and her neck and head were not as large. Otherwise she looked just like Grizzly. I brought her home and provided a place for her in the garage.

A few months later my daughters helped me deliver nine golden retriever puppies. As the puppies were born, I couldn't help but ask the question: "Girls, if you and I can get so excited over the birth of puppies, can we not get excited when people find happiness and fulfillment in their lives?" They thought it was an odd way to teach a lesson, but I hope they felt something positive.

The world is full of wonderful, good people. Many are doing the best they can with what they have been given. No, life is not generally fair. No, everything is not equal. But if we do the best we can with what we have, things almost always work out over time. What's wrong with trying to make the world a better place? What's wrong with helping people be happy as they venture through their circle of life? What's so bad about being good and doing good? By "being good" I mean doing unto others as you would have them do unto you; caring for others and their happiness; and finding and living by true and correct principles that apply to all humans regardless of race or religious affiliation.

In the classic movie *Fiddler on the Roof*, Reptevia does not feel that the poor tailor is wealthy enough to marry his daughter, so in frustration the tailor cries out, "Even a poor tailor is entitled to some happiness!" I agree. Everyone on earth is entitled to not just some happiness but a great amount of happiness. Every decision is accompanied by a consequence. Therefore, we must learn to make correct or right decisions based on correct principles. So now, knowing what I mean by being good: What's so bad about being good? What's wrong with being straight? What's wrong with choosing the right?

In the following chapters we will try to establish the philosophy that there is nothing at all bad about being good, whether you be parent or child. In fact, we will discuss the idea that there are literal powers that can come from being good that can come in no other way. Many examples will be shared from the lives of good people, past and present, male and female, young and old, who have been good and who have made a difference in the world. Stories will be shared to fortify and uplift those who are already doing all they can to be good and to help those who have made serious mistakes who desire to redirect their lives so that they can once again believe they are of great worth. We will also discuss how we can build our own self-esteem, as well as the self-esteem of our children and others.

Hopefully each person will not only enjoy this reading experience but also learn from it. Let us join together and explore some of the powers of being good.

Chapter Two

What's So Bad About Being Good?

How many times have you watched the classic film *The Wizard of Oz?* How many times have Dorothy (and Toto too) come into your life? If you're like many people, you have seen it many, many times.

As a young boy I cold hardly wait to watch it during each annual showing on TV. This was long before there were videos to be rented on every street corner. As I grew older and was playing football in college, watching that movie was still enjoyable. It was funny how some of my fellow players would visit me on that night to watch the movie, something they would never own up to around the other players.

I have lost count of how many times I have watched the movie. When videocassette recorders first became popular, my wife and I won one in a drawing at a local video store. Shortly thereafter the movie was on television, and somehow we figured out how to use the machine. When the movie came on wc recorded it on the complimentary videocassette that came with our prize. This was in the days when video machines were not very refined so we got only a rough copy, but no matter.

For about a year *The Wizard of Oz* was the only video we owned. At that time we had three young daughters. Guess what they wanted to watch almost every day we were home? Sometimes on weekends and holidays they would watch it two or three times a day. I can safely say I have watched it a couple of hundred times. I grew to appreciate it in a way I would never have thought possible. Many words from the movie have become bywords in our home. One of our daughters even pretended for about a year that her name was Dorothy; she also named a stuffed animal "Toto too!"

The phrase "Toto too" comes from the scene in which Dorothy is preparing to fly home to Kansas with the wizard in his hot-air balloon. Toto unexpectedly darts after a cat. In the meantime, the Wizard loses control of the balloon and leaves without Dorothy. Glinda (the good witch) floats onto the scene in a large clear bubble. She tells Dorothy she has always had the power to go home, but that in order to do so she had to learn for herself something very important. Dorothy had to learn, that no matter where you go in the world, there is no place like home. Now, with this knowledge, Glinda says, the ruby slippers can take Dorothy home in two seconds. Before clicking her heels together three times, Dorothy asks, "Toto too?" Glinda responds, "Toto too." Even today our family members sometimes kid with one another about "Toto too."

Now, watching a movie a couple of hundred times either bores you or helps you appreciate it more than ever. My experience with *The Wizard of Oz* was that I grew to love it more than ever. Many lessons can be learned from it, and the symbolism is deep. For example: The first few minutes are filmed in black and white, as are the last five minutes. The movie doesn't use full color until Dorothy "leaves" Kansas and goes over the rainbow—she leaves the sheltered environment of Kansas and sees the world from a new perspective.

From the movie's memorable characters can be learned other interesting lessons.

Dorothy is a symbol of a sweet, innocent girl from "Your Town, U.S.A.," who enters a world where the wicked try to capture her and steal her power source, the ruby slippers.

The qualities of the other characters in Dorothy's company suggest another underlying theme of the movie: You are what you think you are. For instance, the Scarecrow is not supposed to have a brain. He has been told and he believes that there is nothing in his head but straw. However, he thinks of every plan during the entire adventure. The Scarecrow has always had a brain, but he has believed people who have told him he has a head full of straw. Later when the Wizard gives him a degree of "Doctor of Thinkology," the Scarecrow instantly raises his finger to his wise head, and quotes a mathematical equation. He simply needed someone to tell him he had a brain. He then believed it himself.

The Tin Man supposedly has no heart, yet he is always being told not to cry or he will rust. The Wizard later hangs a mechanical heart around his neck, and when Dorothy says her final good-byes to her friends the Tin Man tells her, "Now I know I've got a heart, because it's breaking." He always had one. He needed someone to remind him that the love others had for him was proof of his own loving heart.

The Cowardly Lion—my favorite character (I love it when he says, "I do believe in spooks, I do believe in spooks I do, I do, I do, I do, I do)—supposedly has no courage, but once he joins the group, he often leads the way. When he first encounters Dorothy, the Tin Man, the Scarecrow, and Toto, he puts on a display of courage and tries to capture and bite Toto. But his sense of cowardice is soon confirmed when, after Dorothy slaps him on the nose, he cries and carries on, lamenting his lack of courage. Later, after a medal for courage—courage he has shown in things like helping rescue Dorothy—has been pinned to his mane by the wizard, he exclaims, "Ain't it the truth!" Again, when someone believed in him he began to believe in himself.

This is a roundabout way to get to the point, but all these ideas lead up to what, in my opinion, is one of the greatest scenes and lessons taught in motion-picture history.

Dorothy and Toto have been captured by the Wicked Witch and are locked up in a room while an hourglass is quickly draining. Once it is empty, the Witch says, Dorothy will no longer be alive, and the Witch will have the Ruby slippers.

Dorothy's friends help her escape. After they break open the large wooden doors with the Tin Man's ax and give Dorothy some quick hugs, the entire group runs down the stairs to the main court of the castle.

Suddenly their way is cut off when some huge double doors slam shut before them. An evil cackle is heard, and they turn to see that the Witch is standing on a balcony over them. "Going so soon?" she asks them. "I wouldn't hear of it. Why, my little party's just beginning." Several of the Witch's guards appear and surround Dorothy and her friends. (I have always found the guards quite comical. I think that they must love cookies. They march around the castle with their spears, heavy coats, and tall furry hats, chanting something that sounds like "O-re-o, eoh-ah. O-re-o, eoh-ah." Perhaps they are waiting for a cookie break.)

While the Witch laughs in delight, enjoying her apparent victory, the Scarecrow has enough time to think of a plan. He sees a rope leading to a chandelier hanging directly above the guards. He grabs the Tin Man's arm that holds the ax and cuts the rope. The chandelier falls on the guards, a diversion that allows Dorothy and her friends to run to the top of the wall surrounding the castle. But each way they try to run, guards cut them off. Finally they are surrounded once more in a small tower room where burning torches give light and a bucket of water is within Dorothy's reach (of course it was in the script; otherwise Dorothy couldn't have escaped!).

The Wicked Witch enters the tower, again cackling. "Well, ring-around-the-rosy, a pocketful of spears!" she says. "Thought you'd be pretty foxy, didn't you? Well, the last to go will see the first three go before her and her mangy little dog too!"

She then stretches her broom towards the flame of one of the torches. The broom catches fire—the fire is, I believe, symbolic of evil, death, and destruction. She lights the Scarecrow's arm, taunting, "How about a little fire, Scarecrow?"

Dorothy's first reaction is to reach for the bucket of water to put out the fire. The water symbolizes purity, life: it is the cleansing agent, the purifier. As Dorothy grabs the bucket of water, the Witch, in horror, screams, "Don't touch that water!" Splash! The water covers the Witch's face, hands, and torso. As the cleansing solution touches her wickedness, she begins to melt. She whines, "Oh, what a world, what a world! Who would have thought a good little girl like you could destroy my beautiful wickedness!"

What a deep thought! It must be repeated: "Oh, what a world, what a world! Who would have thought a good little girl like you could destroy my beautiful wickedness!" She then melts away. As smoke arises from the black heap of her clothing, a guard declares, "Hail to Dorothy! The Wicked Witch is dead!" One good girl destroyed all the "beautiful" wickedness in an entire land.

Oh, what a world, what a world we live in! Is there a lot of wickedness and corruption? Can one good boy or girl, man or woman, help in destroying it? If you and I are good, and live according to true, correct, and time-tested principles, can we really make a difference and help destroy some of the "beautiful wickedness?

The answer is a resounding yes! Then my next question is: What's so bad about being good? What's wrong with being clean, virtuous, and doing what's right? What's wrong with living productive lives that not only benefit ourselves but all those around us? What's wrong with teaching these principles to our own children and other young people? Many *believe* in proven traditional values. They *believe* in helping others in times of need and in being kind but do they express these beliefs by their actions or just include them in their belief systems. What's wrong with incorporating these values and principles into our everyday choices? What's wrong with being good? Often, as I travel and speak to various groups of youth and adults, I hear some interesting arguments about being "*too* good." Many say, "It's okay to be good. But don't be too good or people will think you're weird or a geek or a goody-goody."

I wonder how many of the great men and women in history responded to their peers? Were they *too* good? Many, like Christ, Abraham Lincoln, and Joan of Arc, lost their lives because of their goodness. What about all the unknowns who lived quiet lives of service, who blessed countless people and died without fortune and fame? They were just simply good. What about them? What about the countless millions who have given their lives to preserve freedom for others they never knew or met? Why did they do it? Because most of them were good and wanted all people to have freedom to choose how they would live. They were good! To them, helping others was worth the ultimate sacrifice, the laying down of one's life for another. Let me illustrate this point with a very personal story.

The years 1941 to 1945 brought much sorrow to the small town where my mother and father were raised. Although in many ways this town was not much different than most rural American towns during the early 1940s the area did suffer an unusually high death rate of servicemen during the Second World War. In this town, very few lives were untouched, and almost everyone in town lost a family member or friend to the cause of freedom. My family was no exception.

To this day my father feels deeply the loss of his cousin "Big Chris," Allen Christianson. "Big Chris" was flying in a P-38 in North Africa; one day his plane collided with a B-17 bomber while landing. Chris did not survive the crash. Each Memorial Day I walk with my dad to Chris's grave and place flowers near his headstone. Each year I hear the same story and see the same sorrow in my father's eyes as he recounts what happened and as he remembers the good times they had before the war separated them.

Each year as we drive into the cemetery, we gaze at the many, many white crosses positioned in dozens of straight rows. Each cross honors a serviceman or woman from that town who gave his or her life for freedom or who served in the armed forces and died later of other causes.

Positioned in those rows are two crosses that have very special significance to my mother's family. These crosses bear the names of her two older brothers, Franklin and Ralph. Both saw action in the South Pacific. Franklin was killed aboard the USS *Walk,* a naval destroyer, and Ralph served on the USS *Talladega.* Ralph did not die until the 1970s, but the two brothers' lives were very much entwined in January 1945. Franklin served as an officer, and Ralph was a signalman. Both of their ships were engaged in the battle of Lingayen Gulf.

The *Talledega* was a troopship trying to land troops on a beach, and the *Walk* was a destroyer in a fleet of American ships providing protection for the troops so they could successfully take the beach and fulfill their mission. The casualty rate of those landing on the beach from the troopships was extremely high. All aboard knew that chances of survival were slim to none, but they bravely attempted to fulfill their missions in order to provide freedom for future generations. On a typical beach landing, a casualty rate could be as high as 85 percent for the first wave of soldiers and marines and 50 percent for the second wave. It is difficult to imagine what went through the minds of these valiant men as they contemplated giving their young lives so others might be free. Perhaps the scripture referred to in Chapter One filled some of their minds and hearts: "Greater love hath no man than this, that a man lay down his life for his friends" (John 15:13).

The battle that Franklin and Ralph were engaged in had been going on for some six days. The Japanese had been making air strikes, and the USS *Walk* had done everything it could to protect the *Talledega* or other ships. On the sixth day of the battle, six Japanese suicide bombers attempted an attack. Five were shot down before they reached any ships; the sixth, evidently realizing it would never reach the *Talledega* or other troopships, decided to blow up the *Walk*. As the pilot flew his plane towards the deck of the *Walk,* Franklin stood on the bridge watching a young teenage gunner firing in the direction of the oncoming plane. The tracer bullets were not being fired anywhere near the oncoming plane, and Franklin knew that if the plane released its bomb and hit the ship, the entire crew could be killed, leaving one less destroyer to protect the troopships.

In an instant, Franklin did his duty as an officer: he ran from the bridge to the antiaircraft gun, threw the young sailor down some stairs to safety, and began firing at the suicide bomber.

The pilot was shot and killed before he could release the bomb, but Franklin could not stop the plane from hitting the ship. He kept firing to the very end. The plane hit the ship right where Franklin was standing, killing him instantly. The ship survived because the bomb on the plane did not explode. The young teenage gunner survived because he was thrown to safety. Ralph and the *Talledega* survived because the suicide planes never reached their decks. But Franklin lost his life in preserving others' lives. He died a hero. A true hero. He was buried at sea, and none of his family or friends ever saw his remains. His beautiful wife, daughter, and unborn son were left without their hero so others might be free. He laid down his life for his friends. He died not only for his friends, but also for his brother on the *Talledega.* He not only laid down his life for Ralph, but for you and me as well.

Each time I enter the cemetery in my parents' hometown, these events come to mind. Of course, I can't share all that happened and how the lives of the teenage gunner and my uncle Ralph turned out, but their lives were forever altered that January day in 1945. The lives of my grandparents, my mother, my uncles and aunt, and now yours and mine, cannot and never will be the same.

Are we living good, honest, moral lives so we can show our gratitude for all the Franklins who have willingly given their lives so you and I can worship in our own way or believe whatever we want to believe? Or have we given these type of things and people very little thought or appreciation? Most who will live on planet Earth will never hear the name of my Uncle Franklin, but his good life has influenced many in many ways. Someone once said, "America is great because America is good. If America ceases to be good, America will cease to be great!"

With that thought, again, the question must be asked: What's wrong with being clean and wholesome? Why do some people keep thinking that being straight is being strange?

Some argue that if you're "too good," you are hypocritical or you have a "holier-than-thou" outlook. I just don't agree. Being good, as we have defined goodness, should lead to the opposite of a "holier-than-thou" attitude. To me, being good means that instead of feeling that "I'm better than someone else," I must respect each individual as a person of great and infinite value and worth; thus, that individual is my equal and perhaps my superior in at least one vital way.

Sure, we may encounter plenty of hypocrites and self-righteous people in our dealings with others. Why should that stop or hinder us from being all we should be? It's not the hypocrite's life. We can't spend our time and energy worrying about things over which we have no control. We can't walk around waiting for someone to disagree with us or to offend us—I can't anyway. I haven't got time or energy enough to get my feelings hurt if others are hypocrites. Why should we allow a few self-righteous people to determine our worship, lifestyle, or happiness?

Yes, some people don't live up to what they teach or preach. They suffer from the same problem you and I do: they're mortals! They make mistakes! It will always be thus. Our goal is to do the best we can with what we have and try and help others do the same. We must lift and inspire, not spend our lives trying to find fault in others.

Let us allow God to take care of those who claim to be better than others, and let us take care of ourselves, remembering and striving to live according to our values and principles. Something that has been helpful to me along these lines is to always try to remember my name and my family. I was named with the same name as my father and don't want to do anything that would bring shame to his name. Each time I hear my name, I am reminded of what is expected of me and what kind of man I should be while living and working in a world of imperfect mortals. I am often brought back to the teachings of my youth and childhood. I want to honor and respect my name and what my family represents. I want to be good!

Have you ever been sitting at a funeral and heard people say things about the deceased that you knew were not true? Most of us have on one occasion or another. It's uncomfortable, isn't it? You look at others and smile, wondering if you're at the right funeral. If you are like me, don't you wonder what people will say at your funeral. Will anybody even attend the service? What will people say about you when you are dead? Will it be the truth or will it be difficult to find anything good to say? Will the speakers have to make things up? It's a sobering thought, isn't it?

A good friend of my wife summed it up just about perfectly prior to her death from cancer. Her life hadn't turned out the way she had hoped. She had tried to do everything right according to her value system. She had married her Prince Charming, had a family, served in her church and community, taught elementary school, did everything she could to have things turn out the way she had always dreamed as a young girl. Then her husband left her for another woman, leaving her to raise her family alone. If that were not enough, she was diagnosed with a terminal case of cancer. But she never quit believing that she should be good. She did the best she could with what

21

she had. She wrote this little piece just prior to her death; it inspires me when people scoff at the idea of being good.

> I don't want to drive up to the Pearly Gates in a shiny sportscar, wearing beautifully tailored clothes, with my hair expertly coiffed and with long, perfectly manicured nails. I want to drive up to the Pearly Gates in a station wagon that has Boy Scout equipment in the back seat. I want there to be grass stains on my shoes from mowing Mrs. Schneck's lawn. I want there to be a smudge of peanut butter on my shirt from making sandwiches for a sick neighbor's children. I want there to be a little dirt under my fingernails from helping 4-H'ers plant a garden. I want there to be childrens' sticky kisses on my cheeks and the tears of a friend on my shoulder. I want God to know that I was really here and that I really lived.

What an attitude! When you die, will God know that you were really here and you really lived? How will he know? Will there be dirt under your fingernails or grass stains on your shoes? Will there be sticky kisses on your cheeks or tears of a friend on your shoulders? Or will there be no proof that you were here because you did so little good that no one else's life was affected, because all you thought about was yourself? Hopefully there will be volumes of good that will prove you were really here and that you really lived. Be assured that one good boy or girl, man or woman, can and will make a difference in this world.

Chapter Three

One Is Often a Multitude

As we concluded the last chapter, we came to the determination that one good girl, boy, man, or woman can truly make a difference. The list of good individuals who have greatly influenced the world is long. Undoubtedly, each of us has a personal hero or heroine who has motivated us to do our best and to be our best. Are all the heroes gone? Do they exist only in the pages of books or on TV and movie screens? With some time and concentration, we could list many who have influenced great numbers of people.

Now, perhaps you or I may never be great in the eyes of the world or influence great multitudes of people; perhaps our names will never be etched in the pages of history; our words may never be quoted; we may never write a bestseller or be a movie or sports star. But what if we quietly live out our lives doing the best we can? What if we are just good, committed moms and dads, sons and daughters, brothers and sisters? What if we simply become good neighbors and loyal friends? What if we never become the president or CEO of a corporation? What if we become just simple, down-to-earth people with our heads on straight and our priorities in order?

What would happen to our world, our nation, our communities, and our homes if we each were just patient, honest, and kind? What would transpire if we became honest bankers, car sales people, business people, construction workers, teachers, actors, musicians, lawyers, and so on? If people started caring about each other, what would happen to many of our social problems and challenges? Would the world be influenced for good? Of course it would.

Many readers may think that I must live in a dream world to think that people could actually live this way, but think about it: this world would and could change if we all (or even a few of us) cared about being good. I believe in the adage "One is often a multitude." I also love Gandhi's statement: "My life is my message." We don't need to talk a big show, we just need to live the values we espouse. We need to teach our values all the time and if necessary, use words. Hopefully, by letting our lives be our message, we will believe and understand that being good makes a difference, and that fame and fortune are not prerequisites to influencing people.

Each Christmas many of us enjoy watching the classic film *It's a Wonderful Life,* starring Jimmy Stewart, as George Bailey and Donna Reed, as his faithful wife. George feels his life has been a failure because he never pursued his dream to become an architect and travel the world. He simply lived his life out in the same little town where he was born, and there he helped his friends and loved ones fulfill their dreams.

After losing the money he needed to maintain his business, George feels his life has been a waste, so he decides to end it by jumping off a bridge into a river. He is saved by an angel named Clarence, who tries to convince George that he really has had a "wonderful life." Clarence shows him a vision of what would have happened if George Bailey had never lived. In the vision George's brother drowned at age four, because George wasn't there to save him; he would never grow up to be a war hero. George's wife never married but lived alone and unhappy, and their children were never born because George wasn't there. The local pharmacist went to prison then became a drunk because George wasn't there to correct his potentially harmful mistake in filling a prescription. Many townspeople never purchased or built homes of their own because George Bailey wasn't there to loan them money through the savings and loan association. Finally, George recognizes that his is a "wonderful life." His little good deeds have affected the lives of many other good people.

Like George, many of us may feel our lives are not very important to the entire scheme of things in this huge universe. The next time you begin to feel like you make little difference, stop and consider all those whose lives would be different if you did not exist as the unique individual you are. Some of you may even feel that others would be better off without you around—before you fall into that trap, remember George Bailey! He had no way of knowing he was influencing so many. You don't either! You must not lose hope. You must not give up. You do make a difference. You just may need a Clarence in your life to help you see more clearly. That's why this book has been written: Its purpose is to help everyone realize and believe that their individual life, when lived according to true and correct principles, has a profound impact on all of us. None of us knows the future. How do we know our lives today are not influencing future generations?

Consider the story told in Genesis 18 of the Old Testament. Abraham, upon understanding God's plan to destroy the wicked cities of Sodom and Gomorrah, asks a serious question: "Wilt thou also destroy the righteous with the wicked?" Abraham then begins an intriguing series of questions: He asks if the two cities could be preserved if there could be found fifty righteous (good) within Sodom. God's response is that if fifty could be found then He would preserve the cities.

After this interchange, Abraham becomes bolder. He lowers the number to forty-five, then to forty. Still God agrees to save everyone in both cities if just forty "good" people, young or old, could be found. Abraham then asks about thirty, then twenty, and finally ten.

God was willing to save every single person if only ten "good" people could be found. There was only one major problem: ten could not be found. The result? God rained brimstone and fire down upon Sodom and Gomorrah, and all the residents but Abraham's nephew Lot and his two daughters were destroyed.

What a tragedy! A few good people could have saved two entire cities. A few good people really can make a difference.

The next time any of us want to make fun of or gossip about those who appear to be "goodie-goodies," or whatever we call them, perhaps we should fall to our knees and thank them for having the courage to be good. Their good lives may be the only reason our city or town is still on the map! Kind of a scary thought, isn't it? Perhaps the only reason some of us are still alive today is because some teenage boy or girl is not ashamed to be made fun of, and all the rest of us are the beneficiaries.

Does being good make a difference? How can mere words on a page even begin to express what a difference it makes? To those of you who are trying to be good, no matter how hard it gets, I say thank you. Also, I say to you that it is worth it. Your life and goodness are making a difference.

To those of you who may have slipped and wondered if there is a way to find peace and happiness, please keep trying. You can and will make it. It is worth every effort and every pain.

To those of you who have lost hope and are discouraged, it is not too late. Do whatever it takes to change your life now. Do it right now, this minute. If that means getting on your knees and asking for help, do it now. If it means asking someone for forgiveness or asking for help from someone you trust, do it now. Don't wait for everything to be perfect before you start.

Start now! If you need to get into a treatment program or to take medication, then start today. Don't wait until you hit rock bottom, it isn't necessary. Do whatever it takes to be good. Eat your pride if necessary, but start today!

The greatest contribution any of us can make toward personal, community, family, or world peace is to live a good clean life and then help those who will listen to do the same. Happiness is inseparably connected with decent, clean behavior, and behavior is greatly improved when linked to standards and values. It has been my experience that practical values applied to everyday life produce positive results in individuals, families, communities, and countries.

At the beginning of this chapter it was mentioned that most likely each of us has a hero or heroine who has motivated us to be better. There are many, both ancient and modern, in my personal hall of fame; in fact, if I were to write about cach of them, it would fill an entire book. Most of those who have deeply influenced my life can be read about in the pages of history and Scripture. However, some that will be mentioned in this book are likely to be unknown to most readers. That is why they are so significant: Most people have never heard of them yet they had a profound impact on the world in which they lived. With their goodness, they destroyed a whole lot of wickedness. Only a few will be listed here, in the hope that they will influence your life in some degree, as they have mine: perhaps they can give you hope and encouragement as well. Some on my list have become great and famous. Others have lived simple, almost unnoticeable lives. The common thread that binds them all together is that each was or is good. Each was just one good boy, girl, man, or woman. A few made decisive changes in their lives in order to turn them to good.

Again, keep in mind that a full list would be long. Only few can be discussed on these pages. These individuals are not listed in order of their importance.

1.

The first person on my list remains unknown to me by name. I observed her some years ago when my wife and I took our children to a Special Olympics track meet. We wanted our children to gain an appreciation of and love for those less fortunate than themselves. We knew that the Special Olympians are people with great spirits and treasures on the inside who happen to have mental or physical handicaps; despite their outward appearances or abilities, they are real people with real feelings and real needs. Though none of these athletes will ever be famous or go down as champions in the record books of the world, they are all champions nonetheless, because they do their very best.

We wanted to teach our children this vital lesson about life. We wanted them to know that the Special Olympics motto is not just for Special Olympians, but a tremendous motto for success in life. It is: "Let me win. But if I cannot win, let me be brave in the attempt." We may not always be the very best or always win, but we can always be brave. We hoped our children would learn to not fear and to have faith that they can be brave and face anything life has to offer. What we all gained was an example to follow in everything we must face in our lives.

The track meet proved to be the teacher we hoped it would be. Our children loved it once they got used to the open show of affection and the athletes' mannerisms. They watched the "huggers" hug every participant after each event. They felt the love and warmth of athletes and volunteers. However, the most significant lesson came with the women's 100-meter dash.

One of the participants was a woman in her twenties with Down's syndrome. She appeared to be as wide as she was tall. She obviously had split her pants seams, and the large safety pin fastened in the front was a futile attempt to keep the pants together and on her body.

When the starting gun was fired, the runners took off; the woman with the safety pin was dead last. Her thighs were so large that it was difficult for her to get one leg in front of the other, but she persisted. Then it happened: The safety pin popped, the pants fell to her ankles, and she ran two more difficult steps before falling flat on her face.

I wanted to jump from the stands and help her. Before I could move, however, she stood up, pulled up her pants, held them together in front with one hand, and hobbled to the end of the track. When she crossed the finish line she fell into the outstretched arms of a hugger. Everyone cheered for her as if she had won the race. Tears welled up in my eyes as I witnessed such courage. I knew that if this had happened to me I would have found a place to hide rather than finish the race.

That is not the end of the story, however. When the medals were being awarded she stood on the platform, still holding her pants together with one hand. When presented with her medal, she bent over so it could be placed around her neck. As she stood up straight the excitement of having a medal was evidently too much for her to bear, for she raised both hands above her head in triumph and waved excitedly to the crowd, forgetting all about her pants. They fell to her ankles again. She didn't seem to mind that she stood before the large crowd in her underwear. She had done her best and been brave in the attempt.

Hopefully the feelings of that day will never be forgotten. We had watched a true champion, one who did the best she could do. We had been taught by a mentally and physically challenged woman who had no idea she was teaching my family. She lived her life and her life was her message. She didn't have to speak; her message came through clearly. She wasn't trying to teach or influence for good, she just did! I learned to just do my best, and I don't have to compare myself with anyone else. Just be the best you can be with what you have and you will be a great success. Hopefully, in the future, this lesson will sink deep into the hearts of our children; hopefully, it will help you, the reader, to believe in just doing the best you can do.

2.

The late Mother Teresa of Calcutta was an inspiration to many. Joyfully, I watched her on news broadcasts. She spent her entire adult life giving to and sharing with others, showing the entire world that one "good girl" can influence countless millions for good. Again, she didn't do anything to be noticed; she simply cared about relieving human suffering and bringing joy and happiness into the lives of others. She had a special gift for blessing the less fortunate and the downtrodden. She wrote: "We must not drift away from the humble works, because these are the works nobody will do. It is never too small. We are so small we look at things in a small way. But God, being almighty, sees everything great. Therefore, even if you write a letter for a blind man or you just sit and listen, or you take the mail for him, or you visit somebody or bring a flower to somebody—small things—or wash clothes for somebody, or clean the house. Very humble work, that is where you and I must be. For there are many people who can do big things. But there are very few people who will do the small things." (Mother Teresa of Calcutta, *Love: A Fruit Always in Season*, ed. Dorothy S. Hunt [San Francisco: Ignatius Press, 1986], p.26.)

I once read about Mother Teresa sheltering a dying derelict whose body was crawling with worms—she said it took three hours to pick all the worms from his body. She said the emaciated man murmured gratefully that he had lived like an animal but could now die like an angel. She then related how he went home to God with a joyful heart because he had received tender love and care.

Even if Mother Teresa didn't affect millions for good she made a difference in the life of the worm ridden man. Would you have had the stomach and the patience to sit for three hours and remove worms from a derelict's dirty, smelly, body? I would like to think I would, but I don't know. What an example of feeling that every person has value and there is nothing to small when it comes to being good and helping people have dignity and relieve human suffering.

3.

Back in the 1980s I had a student who had a profound impact on me and on many others who knew him. Again, most readers of this book will not ever have heard of him. He was somewhat disruptive in class at times, yet he was so fun to be around that it was difficult to get mad at him. He liked to call me by my first name just to see if he could get a rise out of me. His strategy often worked. At times he drove me crazy.

One time after he had graduated from high school, I was shopping with my family in a local mall. I had no idea that he was working in one of the stores. He saw me coming and hid behind a rack of clothes until I walked by. He ran from behind the clothes and jumped onto my back. He started to laugh when he realized he had caught me by complete surprise. I fell to the floor and he rubbed his knuckles back and forth across my head. For someone who is bald on top, it hurts! He laughed until he was sick. It was quite funny for everyone who saw it.

That was the last time I saw him alive. Steven Eugene Blake met a tragic death in 1988 while saving the life a person whom, to my knowledge, he had never met before. I keep a copy of his obituary in my speaking notes and look at it nearly every week. It may sound a bit strange to carry a copy of a former student's obituary, but it helps me keep focused on why I do what I do each day, what my motives are, and the value of the individual.

Steven was only twenty-one and his whole life lay before him. Yet one decision to serve another ended his young, promising life.

A man was working on an electrical sign when the boom on the truck that was holding up the sign knocked a high voltage wire down onto him. Steven and his friends saw the accident occur and ran to the scene to assist the man, who was being electrocuted. Evidently, Steven didn't hesitate to remove the man from the powerline. But as he grabbed hold of the man and pulled him away, electricity running through the man's body jolted Steven back into the truck, which threw him forward onto the very line from which he had just pulled the worker. Steven was severely burned and died a few days later at local hospital.

He had given the ultimate sacrifice—his life. Why? To save the life of a stranger—a man in his seventies who had just remarried and who was the father of a young child. It will be a long time before I forget the news broadcast showing the man weeping in gratitude. "Why would a young man with his whole life ahead of him do a thing like this for an old man like me?" he asked, his voice choked with emotion.

Steven lived what he believed. Oh, I realize he wasn't perfect. I knew him very well, not only as one of his teachers at school but as his neighbor as well. I'm not trying to paint him bigger than life. I'm just saying he knew that giving his life for a "friend" was the greatest form of love.

I realized that warm, fall day in 1988 that Steven's motives were pure. He did what he did for love and for no other reason.

Is that why you and I serve or want to be good? Do we do it for love, without concern about whether we are recognized or paid back for our efforts? What are our motives for the good we do in our lives?

At the graveside, I watched the pallbearers cry as they placed Steven's casket on the green straps over the grave. I watched his family agonizing over the loss of a beautiful son and brother. One of the pallbearers approached me, put his arms around me, and said, "Isn't it tragic that something like this has to happen to make us realize what really is important in life?"

I've never forgotten that true comment. It is tragic that we must be shaken by death and tragedy to keep us focused on the truly important things. Steven Blake's obituary constantly reminds me to do things for love.

4.

Stillman Pond was an early nineteenth century pioneer who brought his family west from Hubbardston, Massachusetts. In September 1846 Stillman, his wife Maria and their children became part of the great western migration. The early winter that year brought extreme hardships, including malaria, cholera, and consumption. The family was visited by all three of these diseases.

Maria contracted consumption, and all of the children were stricken with malaria. Three of the children died while moving through the early snows. Stillman buried them on the plains. Maria's condition worsened because of the grief, pain, and the fever of malaria. She could no longer walk. Weakened and sickly, she gave birth to twins. Both little boys died within a few days. The Stillman Pond family spent the winter in Nebraska. Like many other families, they suffered bitterly while living in a tent. The death of the five children coming across the plains to Nebraska was but the beginning. Journal accounts verify the following regarding four more of the children of Stillman Pond who perished. "On Wednesday the 2 of December 1846, Laura Jane Pond, age 14 years, . . . died of chills and fever." Two days later on "Friday, the 4 of December 1846, Harriet M. Pond, age 11 years, . . . died with chills." Three days later, "Monday the 7 of December 1846, Abigail A. Pond, age 18 years, . . . died with chills. Just five weeks later, Friday, the 15 of January, 1847 Lyman Pond, age 6 years, died with chills and fever. Four months later, on the 17 of May, 1847, his wife Maria Davis Pond also died. Crossing the plains, Stillman Pond lost 9 children and a wife. He became an outstanding colonizer and a great leader in the west. Having lost these nine children and his wife in crossing the plains, Stillman Pond did not lose his faith nor desire to live and to do good. He did not quit. He went forward and made the best out of a horribly, tragic situation. His example of goodness in the midst of indescribable heartache and tragedy served my family well when we lost our son and brother in the fall of 1989. We learned to move forward and not quit though our hearts seemed to burst with pain and suffering.

5.

In his book, *The Moral Compass,* William J. Bennett retells the ancient, moving story of The Wives of Weinsberg. These women deeply influenced their world with their fidelity and their goodness. Unknowingly their act of selfless service to their husbands influenced for good, countless individuals for future generations. As far as we know, their thoughts were not centered on all the people they would be able to bless by being good. They just wanted to help those whom they loved. The result however, has helped many of us, myself included, never to be the same.

The story takes place in Germany in 1141. Wolf, the Duke of Bavaria, was trapped inside his castle of Weinsberg. Outside the castle the army of Frederick the Duke of Swabia and his brother, the emperor Conrad waited to destroy Wolf. The siege had lasted long, and the time had come when Wolf knew he must surrender. Messengers rode back and forth, terms were proposed, conditions allowed, arrangements completed. Sadly Wolf and his officers prepared to give themselves to their bitter enemy.

However, the wives of Weinsberg were not ready to give up all that they held dear. They sent a message to Conrad, asking the emperor to allow all the women safe passage out of the castle, that they might come out with as many of their valuables as they could carry. Konrad granted their request. The castle gates were opened. Out came the women carrying their most valuable possessions. The armies of Konrad and Frederick were stunned. For the women carried not gold or jewels. Each one was bending under the weight of her husband, whom she hoped to save from the vengeance of the conquering emperor.

Evidently, Konrad's heart was touched and the story records that he was brought to tears by the extraordinary performance. With his generous and merciful nature he assured the women of their husbands' perfect safety and freedom. The Duke of Bavaria, his men and their wives were all invited to a banquet and peace was negotiated on much more favorable terms than was expected.

The castle mount was afterwards known as the Hill of *Weibertreue,* or woman's fidelity.

These women must be included in the list of heroes and heroines because they understood the value of family and other personal relationships over worldly possessions. Seasoned warriors and bitter enemies melted with their example of goodness. Goodness, fidelity, and loyalty made the difference.

As this necessarily short and incomplete list of heroes and heroines comes to a conclusion I would like to mention just a couple of others. I marvel at the great influence for good that many of my school teachers and religious leaders have had and continue to have on my life. Their simple yet great examples of patience, love and determination have helped me strive to be the same kind of teacher and leader. Often I wonder why some of these teachers did not give up on me. Perhaps they could see something I could not see. Today when entering a classroom, I finally understand. As I look into the sea of student faces, some appear to have my young face. I then think back and try harder not to give up on those who fight so defiantly not to be taught.

On a more personal level, I can't help but think of how my good grandparents have influenced their many descendants. They were good, simple people who lived most of their lives in a rural community never traveling much or acquiring great wealth or fame. Of course they weren't perfect, but I will praise their names forever.

And lastly, the list cannot be concluded without mentioning my parents. They too were not perfect, but they were always good parents and friends to me. They gave me life. Perhaps I can use what they taught me to bless many other lives. The day I left home for the first time, they gave me some advice I have used and never forgotten. Paraphrasing what I was told, "Son, if you will always give part of what you earn back to God and love people, you will be a successful man." I have lived to see the validity of that advice. By recognizing that everything we have and are and ever will be comes from a power higher than ourselves and loving each human being, not only will we destroy a lot of wickedness in the world we live in, but we will influence for good many others, helping them to see that this truly is a "wonderful life".

Chapter Four

The Interruption

During my first year of teaching high school, I walked into a fellowteacher's office one afternoon. On the wall was a sign that read, "You are not the interruption of my life, but the purpose for it." The sign did not make sense to me for quite some time. Now, after years of teaching high school and college students, it has become a watchword or a type of mission statement. It has greatly influenced my attitude towards those who frequently come to my office with so many needs. They are young and inexperienced in real life, yet want to know much. Their questions are countless concerning what to study, how to make money, who to date, when or if they should get married, etc.

In their inexperience many seem to think that if teachers are in their offices or not teaching a class that they don't have anything to do, or prepare. Some even ask, "Why do you need to prepare? You've taught long enough that it just happens, doesn't it?" I wish! In order to stay fresh and current, daily preparation and study is essential. The problem is, if other teachers are like me, they have to hide to do it. There are so many interruptions that it is almost impossible to complete the needed preparation, writing, or stacks of paperwork. In order to avoid "teacher burnout," a teacher must work at "keeping the saw sharp." Teaching is similar to other occupations in that if a teacher spends all of his time "sawing," taking little time to sharpen the saw, he will soon become dull and ineffective in his work. Without this renewal and sharpening process it is easy to become cynical or negative like the longtime teacher who told me my first year that I had made a mistake in becoming a teacher. He said that it is naive to believe that anyone can really make a difference in someone's life by teaching. He went on to tell me to get real and don't have high expectations because the students don't want to learn and that it is a waste of time to try to teach them anything.

When interruptions persist, it is almost impossible to accomplish all there is to do without taking it home, working weekends, or staying well after hours. The countless interruptions that I seem so encounter have caused some fellow teachers to nickname me "The Magnet," and it sometimes seems to fit. It is easy to tire of continually meeting with students and rarely getting to, or having time for my "real work."

One day when I was feeling extremely pressured, with no time for an unscheduled visitor, I had an experience that taught me the meaning of the phrase I had observed years earlier: "You are not the interruption of my life, but the purpose for it." The saying finally made sense. Finally, I understood. Oh, I had learned the lesson many times but now it entered my mind and heart with power. It changed me! I had always believed that people, not things, were important, and I had tried to teach it, but now I truly began to understand. In the midst of all my interruptions the thought came into my mind how sad it would be if students and others never sought my advice or were left with the impression that I had no time for them. I thought about how lonely and disheartened the great baseball player and Hall of Fame superstar Willie Mays must have felt when he said the greatest disappointment in his magnificent baseball career was that, in spite of all his greatness and prowess as a hitter, no young person ever asked him how to hit a baseball. What a tragedy! One of the greatest players of all time and no one ever dared ask how he did it.

Though pressured, I left my office for a drink of water and a quick trip to the restroom. As I came out the door there stood a somewhat dejected-looking student. She was approximately seven months pregnant. She was evidently waiting for one of my colleagues who wouldn't be back in town for two weeks.

She asked if I knew where he was and when he would be back. I told her and then proceeded down the hallway to accomplish my objective. She looked heartsick when I gave her the news, and she started to walk away in quiet misery.

I thought about asking if I could be of assistance but immediately reminded myself that I had a desk full of "work." Besides, I thought, if I could complete the work I would have time to break away that afternoon and get nine holes of golf in with another student. I dismissed the idea. She walked away. Then, before I could stop myself, I called down the hall for her to please wait. I knew the student, but we were not close, by any means, but it was obvious that she was in great emotional pain and needed to talk. I asked if I could help even though I was not the trained therapist my colleague was. I inwardly hoped she would say no so I could get back to my "work." She didn't. She asked, "Are you sure you have time? I don't want to interrupt."

"I have a few minutes. Please come into my office." I listened for the next hour, nervously fidgeting as I worried about the "work" sitting on my desk.

The girl was approximately seven months pregnant and single. She had just returned from seeing her doctor, where she had learned that the baby within her suffered from a rare genetic disorder and would not live more than a few hours after birth, if he lived at all. As I listened, the words of the sign came into my mind. "You are not the interruption of my life, but the purpose for it." As I

41

contemplated the saying, another thought came quietly and peacefully: *This young woman sitting in front of you is your work!* This is why you are here! This is why you teach! She, not the papers (as important and necessary as they may be), is your work. This is what teachers should do. Teaching is about people. It's about living, learning, happiness, joy, fulfillment, and peace.

She finished sharing her story and her fears, then left with tears of gratitude and hope. By having someone to talk with, she could now face another day and succeed. This young woman, and others like her who frequently come and "interrupt," are not the interruption of my life or work but the very purpose for it!

Who are those who are the purpose for your life? Are they the purpose for your life or the interruption of it? Do you take the needed time to listen, to really hear with the heart and not just the ears? Do our most significant others feel like they are interruptions, or do they know they are the purpose for which we live?

Do we as parents sometimes forget the importance of nurturing our children spiritually and emotionally as well as mentally and physically? Do we take time to just listen and understand them, remembering what it was like to be a child or an adolescent? As my wife so often reminds me, "Sometimes you act like you were born at age forty-four." It is so easy to look upon our children's needs as interruptions rather than our most sacred responsibilities. As I once heard a wise man say, "Love is not spelled LOVE, it is spelled TIME." What a simple but profound insight: Our children not only need us, they need our time. If we view them as interruptions, in the future, family, home, and loved ones will simply become interruptions in their lives rather than the major purpose for it.

In our busy and hectic lives, is it asking too much to spend at least as much time planning for our family activities and family success as we do an important meeting at work, how many flowers go into our garden, or what kind of food we'll serve and what friends we will invite to our home to watch the Superbowl or the "March Madness" basketball games?

How much of a major schedule adjustment would it take to spend just one evening a week with our families? Would it hurt any of us to arrange our schedules in order to eat at least a few meals together each week as a family? It seems to have become a dying tradition for families to sit around the kitchen table to laugh, eat, share experiences, and read together without the interruption of television. Sounds old-fashioned, doesn't it? But shouldn't one of the most important pieces of furniture in any home be the kitchen table? Shouldn't the most important room in the house be "the family room?" It matters little the size of the room or the table or if a table is substituted by a small counter—what matters is that we are together and creating memories so that all individuals can say with Dorothy, "There's no place like home." With this feeling of belonging comes an increase in self-esteem and an opportunity to teach and pass on family values and traditions that create stability in the future. Hopefully, parents and children alike will not look upon family time as an interruption, but as a source of nourishment and strength to better succeed in a hostile world.

Has supporting children at ballgames, concerts, debates, school plays, etc., become an interruption or a parental purpose? Being a parent takes time, effort, and energy: Parenting is not for wimps! It is not for the faint of heart. Because it is demanding, it is easy to look at all the things we are not accomplishing and feel like we are wasting our time, but do our children see it that way? How do they view your efforts to support and sustain them?

The story is told of Charles Francis Adams, the grandson of the second president of the United States. He was a successful lawyer, a member of the U.S. House of Representatives, and the U.S. Ambassador to Britain, and a very busy man. However, he kept a diary, and on one occasion he wrote of going fishing with his son; he recorded that he felt it was a wasted day.

On the same day, Charles's son Brooks wrote in his journal that fishing with his father that day was the most wonderful day of his life. To a busy father, being with his son was a waste of time; to an admiring son, being with his father was the greatest experience of his life.

As a senior in high school I sometimes had different feelings than Brooks Adams. I was somewhat embarrassed to have my mom come to my ballgames because she was so loud. She would always scream at the top of her lungs, "Come on Jack! You can do it, Jack! That's my boy!" I was mortified. My dad usually wouldn't sit by her because he was embarrassed. He would always find a reason to move. He would come to the sideline or to the dugout; he would buy popcorn or a drink. She didn't care. She would sit toward the top of the stands so she could stand up. Whenever I did anything noteworthy, or when I was about to come to bat, she always let me and everyone else know I that I could do whatever needed to be done.

Then one spring afternoon, my feelings changed. It was an intense baseball game. Our team was behind the entire game until we scored four runs in the last inning. Finally, at the end of regulation play the score was tied. The game went into extra innings, and the other team scored two runs.

When we finally got them out, we all gathered in the dugout and vowed that we wouldn't lose and that no one would strike out. (I could talk real big because I was the sixth batter up—I didn't think I'd get a chance to make any difference.)

The first two batters struck out. We then somehow managed to score two runs to tie the score again. It was a Roy Hobbs—Kurt Gibson moment. I came to the plate with two outs, one man on base, and the score tied in extra innings. This was something I had dreamed about all my life. I had a chance to be the hero or the goat.

As I walked to the plate, butterflies were swarming in the pit of my stomach! My hands were sweating and my heart was almost in the batter's box, when my mother stood up and screamed, "Come on Jack! You can do it, Jack. You can do it! That's my boy!" I wanted to hide behind the umpire.

I looked at her with a glare that said, "Please love me enough to be quiet." It didn't work. I hoped that my dad would sense my discomfort and, just this once, get Mom to sit down and be quiet, but Dad had found some other errand in the park; he wasn't anywhere near her.

I battled the pitcher to a full count, three balls and two strikes. The intensity couldn't have been greater in a movie! I battled and battled. Two strikes, two outs, one man on base: I could bring in the winning run. After several foul balls, the opposing coach called time-out. He signaled to the bull pen, and one of the star relief pitchers trotted to the mound. All he had to do was throw one strike.

All during the new pitcher's warm-up, my mother was yelling that I didn't need to worry. That was easy for her to say; she didn't have to try to hit that little white dot.

The umpire finally signaled us to play ball. Now I called a time-out and used the break to hit my cleats with the bat.

45

I didn't really think about why I did that; I had seen Reggie Jackson do it in many tight situations, so I did it. Then I dug my right foot into the ground and touched the end of the bat to the corner of the plate, and my mom yelled again, "Come on, Jack. You can do it, Jack!"

I was so frustrated that I stepped out of the box and glared at her in disgust. She glared back with her fists clenched and shaking in my direction. I don't know what happened at that moment, but my relationship with that dear woman has never been the same since. I realized, for the first time in my young eighteen years, that my mother loved me so much that she wasn't afraid of making a fool of herself in front of the entire crowd in order to show me.

I felt the adrenaline pump through my system. I knew I was going to hit that ball. I was going to show my mom that I could do it! And yes, I was her boy and proud of it!

I stepped into the box with a newfound confidence, looking for an inside fastball. For some reason, the pitcher threw me a slow-breaking curveball. It had my name on it! As it broke, I crunched it down the left-field line. It had enough on it to be a home run, but it went foul!

Talk about pressure! Now I was going to swing, no matter what. If the ball went twenty feet high, I'd throw my bat at it. I was going to hit that ball.

The pitcher wound up and let it rip: It was the same pitch. I couldn't believe it. I waited a split second longer than I had before, and then made solid contact. I still remember standing at home plate, my arms raised in triumph, as I watched the ball sail over the left centerfield fence. I proudly trotted around the bases, knowing that I was the hero.

But what happened as I came back to home plate floored me. There, in the middle of my ecstatic teammates, was my mother. I don't know how she got there so quickly without throwing her back out, but there she was, jumping up and down and screaming.

After all the hoopla at home plate, she grabbed me and twirled me around, all the time kissing me and whispering, "I knew you could do it, son. I knew you could do it." Then she humbled me to tears. As I remember it, she said, "But son, I'd love you even if you had struck out." And I knew she did.

My picture was taken for the town newspaper, the crowd soon was gone, and being a hero for a few minutes became a pleasant memory, but my relationship with my mother had changed forever. From that day to this, I can honestly say that I don't remember one disrespectful, rude, or ornery word escaping my lips to that woman. She and my dad have become two of my greatest heroes. Oh, I'm aware of many of their weaknesses, and I know they are far from being perfect, but I am convinced that the reason why I love them so deeply today is that they first loved me. I was not an interruption in their life. Perhaps not everyone who reads this book has been blessed to have a mother or father like mine, or even to have a mother or father at all, but that is not the point. The point is, that afternoon I knew I was not the interruption in their lives but rather one of the purposes for their lives.

Hopefully I will be disciplined enough in the future to not look at students needing to talk as interruption. And hopefully each reader of this book will not consider helping their children to succeed and face life's challenges to be an interruption, but a major purpose for living. Remember: "You are not the interruption of my life, but the purpose for it."

Chapter Five

Parents: Builders of Men and Women

Parenthood is one of the most effective schools in this life. As a young person I really had no idea what it took for my parents to raise five children—two boys and three girls. I knew that I learned from my parents, but it never occurred to me that they might also be learning from their children. Mom and Dad made us feel that each of us was their favorite child. But I was not aware of the sacrifice, tears, prayers, work, inconvenience, time, or energy it took for a construction worker and a full-time homemaker to be such wonderful parents. Neither did it dawn on me that there was both joy and pain in parenthood—until I became a father.

Now, as one who lives daily with teenagers, my love for my mother and father has never been deeper. I think most people find, as I did, that it takes parenthood for us to appreciate what our folks went through. Now I can understand why I cannot express the depth of my devotion to my wife and children in mere words. I have learned far more from them than they from me. Learning that comes in ordinary experiences, the joy and the pain of everyday life. I now understand that the ultimate purpose of every teaching, every activity at home, at school, at work, at play, and at church, should be to ensure that parents and their children are happy at home, with ties to all family members. Everyone belongs to a family even if they are single or never have an opportunity to marry. We all belong somewhere! If we don't have brothers, sisters, mothers, fathers, husbands, wives, or children, we still belong to the human family. We still belong to God. We can belong to a community, church, or other social organization. Again, we all belong! We all deserve some happiness, peace, fulfillment, and joy. On the other hand, it often appears that the ultimate purpose of many people in the world, is to disrupt, disturb, and destroy the home and the family. Like a plane with no instruments, without a guidance system we drift from the family values that have been an anchor in the past. Now we are caught in a nosedive so powerful that, unless we pull out of it, civilization as we know it will surely be wrecked to pieces.

If the tide of evil is to be turned back and our civilization kept from being totally wrecked on the shoals of permissiveness and violence, effective parenting is the answer. We must be parents who build young minds, bodies, and spirits, rather than parents who tear down and destroy. There are no perfect families, but there are many good ones. There are many things we can do to develop a strong home life. Our parental challenge is to build strong family members—individuals who can attract mates and build successful family units of their own. Family relations continue as long as we draw breath. We must be found building and lifting, never giving up or yielding to worldly trends; the educator Neal A. Maxwell has cautioned "that as parenting declines, the need for policing increases. There will always be a shortage of police if there is a shortage of effective parents! Likewise, there will not be enough prisons if there are not enough good homes."

Next to the front door in our home hangs a framed plaque that hopefully has deeply impacted our four daughters throughout their lives. Having all daughters in our home has been quite an experience. Our desire as parents has been to remind them, every time they leave the house, not who they are and what they represent but rather what they were born to be. We also wish to remind every young man who takes them out on a date what they were born to be and how they are expected to be treated. The plaque reads, in beautiful calligraphy, "I was born to be a queen." Every day that our daughters leave the home, for any reason, they are reminded that they were born to be queens. Also, anyone who comes to our home and then leaves through our front door is reminded not only that our daughters were born to be queens but that every human being is born to be a queen or a king. When one comes to realize their infinite worth and the divine within them, this realization changes them. It changes attitudes and behaviors more quickly and profoundly than studying about human behavior can change an individual's behavior. When an individual grows up believing that they have worth, and that dignity, mastery, and control—all three divine attributes—are the guiding principles in their lives, they view life with different eyes. They see setbacks and challenges as but small stepping-stones to their successes. They learn to treat others with dignity, kindness, and compassion.

The idea for the plaque came from a story I read back in 1975 that so profoundly affected me that I wanted it to have the same type of an affect, if possible, on each of my lovely daughters. It is the true story of the son of King Louis XVI of France.

King Louis had been taken from his throne and imprisoned. His young son, the prince, was taken by those who had dethroned the king. They thought that inasmuch as the king's son was heir to the throne, if they could destroy him morally he would never fulfill the great and grand destiny that life had bestowed upon him.

They took him to a community far away, and there they exposed the lad to every filthy and vile thing that life could offer. They exposed him to foods the richness of which would quickly make him a slave to appetite; they used foul language around him constantly; they exposed him to lewd and lusting women; they exposed him to dishonor and distrust. He was surrounded twenty four hours a day by everything that could drag the soul of a man as low as one could slip. For more than six months he was subjected to this treatment—but not once did the young lad buckle under pressure. Finally, after intensive temptation, they questioned him: Why had he not submitted to these things—why had he not partaken? These things would provide pleasure and satisfy his lusts; they were all his. The boy said, "I cannot do what you ask, for I was born to be a king."

What a heroic response! The prince would not give in to all the pressures because he was been born to be a king. We were all born to be kings and queens. We may not have been born of royal lineage but our divine worth testifies of divine parentage. Every man, woman, and child has the inalienable right to be treated and respected as a queen or a king. When they are, they will rise to the divine within them. With this knowledge burning deep within us like the young future king, we need not buckle under pressure. We need not follow the crowd and participate in behaviors and lifestyles that lead to sadness, sorrow, and self-destruction.

A question: where is the most ideal place to learn such worth and such ideology? Where is the greatest teaching ground for youth to learn that they are not only born to be queens and kings but deserve to be treated as such? The answer comes in seven simple letters—THE HOME! Seems kind of simple, doesn't it? The answer to so many of life's complex problems lies in what Dorothy in *The Wizard of Oz* learned: "There's no place like home," and you never need look further than your own backyard to find life's treasures and pearls of great price.

Somehow we must believe that the armor of goodness, integrity, and moral character is not manufactured on an assembly line. It must be hand-made in the home. It appears that we have become so busy in our modern society, and with all the technological advances at our disposal we leave little time to make and put on this armor at home. As a result, many families are divided, disrupted, and filled with sorrow. Regardless of what kind of family we belong to, it can be a happy one. Family happiness is the love story of husbands and wives and parents and children, renewing itself through the ages.

Many readers may find the hair on the back of their necks standing up because of the lack of harmony and love or perhaps even abusive situations that may exist in their homes and families. However, when we come to accept and believe that no matter how we have been treated we are kings, queens, princes, and princesses, and that others are too, we can change the future so that no one need suffer the pain and heartache that we may have suffered.

In the 1990s version of the movie *A Little Princess,* the cold, uncompassionate caretaker of students attending a school for affluent young girls refuses to believe that Sara Crewe, the main character, really is a princess; Sara had always been taught so by her father. He, a wealthy Englishman, has mistakenly been reported as killed in action while at war. As a result of the mistake, and knowing that there will be no more economic remuneration for her, the caretaker of the school banishes Sara to the cold, barren, and foreboding attic. She is forbidden to associate with her schoolmates and forced to work as a slave and perform demeaning labor. Despite the depressing situation Sara finds herself in, she continues to help and serve her fellow classmates, who sneak into her attic room to hear inspiring and exciting stories. She brings them joy when they are struggling. In her hours of physical and emotional need she ministers to them. Sara refuses to believe that she is not a princess.

One evening as Sara is entertaining some of her friends in the attic, Miss Minchin catches them. After dismissing the other girls, she confronts Sara and tries to instill in her the fact that she is nothing but a poor waif with a dark future of hard labor, poverty, and sadness—surely she could not fancy herself a princess now. Sara then becomes Miss Minchin's teacher. She convincingly states, "I am a princess. All girls are. Even if they live in tiny old attics. Even if they aren't pretty, or smart, or young, they're still princesses. All of us. Didn't your father ever tell you that. Didn't he?" The look of anguish in Miss Minchin's eyes and the tears that streak her face tell the tragic story: she had never been taught that she was a princess. Would to God that that would never happen to any boy or girl of any race, color, religion, or land of origin.

As children most of us had the opportunity to build something, didn't we? It may have been a sand castle, a wooden hut or tree house, an underground hut, or a secret hideout of blankets thrown over tables or chairs. I remember all of these, as well as a special fort I built on top of a neighbor's horse stall. It was great fun to create and build something and then pretend we were someone other than ourselves.

However, as time passed we suffered pain and personal loss when the things we had worked so hard on were destroyed or were replaced by homes, roads, or modern buildings. Most of the time, until we grew too old to build and create our fantasy abodes, we would rebuild: I think the joy came in the rebuilding process. Back then, we would say that when we grew up we would create and build real homes, jobs, and relationships. Why should we stop this childlike behavior of building and creating? I believe we were born to create, and I sometimes worry that this child-like joy in building and creating stops when we become adults and parents. However, when we become adults and/or parents we have something greater to create: strong, stable, well-rounded children, our sons and daughters. This then becomes our work as adults and parents. We are in the business of building men and women of character who can lead this world to victory. Jesus of Nazareth was not only a carpenter who built tables, chairs, and houses, but he was also a builder of men and women, not a destroyer. He built character. He built esteem. His life is a great example of one who built and lifted others. His chief way of acting was by persuasion and patience and long suffering, not by coercion and stark confrontation.

Building and lifting others' self-esteem must be considered an art, a sometimes difficult one that requires great effort and sacrifice on the part of the builder. In order to build up others—to become creators rather than demolishers—we must be willing to be hurt and rejected. At times we must stand alone against cultural messages that destroy rather than build, but being a builder or creator is being a giver of life, a giver of hope, a giver of purpose. We must become givers and builders of life, hope, and purpose if we are to maximize self-esteem and personal happiness in our children and in others' children.

Have you noticed that self-esteem is a hot topic these days? There are a multitude of books on the subject.

Seminars abound telling us how to like ourselves and feel good about who we are. Poor self-esteem appears to be present in epidemic proportions, not just with youth but with many adults as well. Apparently many, young and old alike, are unaware of their divine nature and infinite worth. In spite of all the seminars and books on this topic, however, we have missed a very important component of true self-esteem—that which comes from building others up, for it is through the process of lifting others that our own self-worth increases.

Before we discuss how to build self-esteem in others, especially in our own children, it is vital for us to clarify the difference between self-esteem and self-confidence. True self-esteem comes from within. It is a feeling that is based on an understanding that each human being is born to be a king or queen. The knowledge of who we are and of our potential brings a feeling of inner peace, strength, and spiritual perspective that can be gained in no other way.

Self-confidence, on the other hand, is generated from external sources. It generally originates from feedback we receive from others and is usually tied to how well we perform tasks. It is easy to confuse the two, but it is essential to separate them. For example, it is quite possible for an individual to have great self-confidence in the area of athletics or music and yet feel little worth as a human being. I learned this lesson playing college football, where many players had self-confidence but not self-esteem. I noticed that these players were self-deprecating and did not seem to like themselves because of an inability to overcome a particular weakness, such as drinking. But on game day, when they walked onto the playing field, where they had to use their athletic prowess, confidence oozed from every pore. They knew their football, and they had confidence in their ability to perform.

In my case, I learned the difference between these two terms in a different way. I knew from my upbringing that I had significant value, that I was loved, needed, and wanted—hence, my self-esteem was intact at an early age. On the other hand, I have absolutely no self-confidence when it comes to using a sewing machine. Let me explain. I took homemaking as a senior in high school. We were learning how to put a drawstring into a pair of swimming trunks when a very unfortunate accident occurred. I was working the machine with the foot pedal while guiding the top part of the trunks under the fast-moving needle. I have no idea how it happened, but before I took my foot off the pedal my right forefinger made its way under the little metal foot, and the needle went through the flesh three or four times.

I tried not to make a scene, for I knew that my buddies would verbally torture me if they knew what I had done. So, very calmly, I raised my hand and asked Miss Greene to come to my table and informed her that I had a slight problem. I still remember the look on her face and what she said: "Oh my," she laughed, "we do have a problem!" With those words she quickly twisted the wheel on the side of the machine, which pulled the needle out of the finger. She then snipped the thread below the needle and very carefully removed it from my finger.

Unfortunately, the mishap did not remain a secret, and the harassment was unrelenting—I honestly don't care to ever touch a sewing machine again! But I'm comfortable with me as a person. Though my confidence in sewing is non-existent, my self-worth remains intact because I know who I am. I identify with the writer of Proverbs, who wrote "For as he thinketh in his heart, so is he" (Proverbs 23:7).

It is dangerous to buy in to so many of the philosophies existing in our world. Hopefully, we can avoid depending upon the world to tell us whether we have value or not. We cannot allow our self-esteem to be determined by where we are on the ladders of worldly success. We must strive to overcome the philosophy which posits that the only way we can feel worthwhile as individuals is if the numbers of those who rank beneath us in achievement, talent, beauty, or intellect are large enough. We must rejoice in the success of others rather than believing that if others succeed we are failures. If we love principles, stay true to our values and moral compasses, and if we fear what heaven thinks of us more than what men do, we will have self-esteem.

With this simple understanding of the concept of self-esteem versus self-confidence, we begin to see who we really are and who we really can be, and we are ready to learn some basic methods of building self-esteem in others.

Chapter Six

The Power of Being Good: Building Self-Esteem in Others

W hat are the benefits of being good? Why is it so crucial in our daily lives to live by correct and moral principles? I certainly do not have all the answers to such questions; however, there are specific powers and advantages that come from being good which can come in no other way. At first they may appear to be so simple that it is easy to underestimate their significance. As with the list of heroes in Chapter Three, this list of benefits is not complete. But in the following four chapters we will discuss four powers that can, if we allow them, enrich our lives. Each is tied to the other, and each has a specific role in helping us live a quality and productive life. They are: (1) the power of building self-esteem in others; (2) the power of spirituality or the ability to communicate with deity and experience deep feelings; (3) the power to be happy and to be at peace amidst adversity and; (4) the power to resist life-destroying influences.

This chapter will focus on the building of self-esteem in others. The art of building self-esteem in others—and thus developing it in ourselves—may take time. We live in a highly critical society, and old habits often die hard. We must first believe in the infinite worth of every human being and also learn from those around us who have become builders of people. As we watch, learn, lift, and build, we become artists in our own right. Our art, however, is not painting upon canvas, but helping people feel worth, dignity, and self-respect because someone cared. There are twelve specific points that can aid us in the process of becoming builders of self-esteem. As we discuss each of the twelve points, remember that these points are universal and will work in the lives of all people, and especially in the lives of our own children. As we strive to build our own children and other people, that which comes back to us, without being forced, is our own self-esteem.

The twelve simple points are:
1. Put people up, not down.
2. Help others to never fear failure, change, or success.
3. Help others to never fear the truth.
4. Stop calling people names and labeling them with damaging verbal barbs.
5. Talk to family and others as you would to a guest in your home.
6. Help others learn to accept a compliment.
7. Teach people to be the best they can be.
8. Recognize that abnormal or unruly behavior is often a cry for help or a sign of insecurity.
9. Help others feel a sense of belonging.
10. Recognize the difference between adolescence and an adolescent.
11. Make a valiant effort to learn and use people's names.
12. Help others to be good by maintaining moral standards and values.

This list is not all-inclusive or necessarily in order of importance. The last point, however, is the very key to self-esteem; without it, true self-esteem, that deep inward feeling of divine worth, cannot be fully felt.

1.
Put people up, not down.

We have become masters of the put-down. Put-downs, negative comments, and sarcastic toasts form the basis of much
that passes for humor. Comedians make millions and car-
toonists make a living being critical and satirical toward
public figures and various cultures. Sarcasm, it seems, has
become a way of life. When will we learn that biting sarcasm undermines meaningful relationships—sacred relationships between parents and children and neighbors and
friends? Criticisms and put-downs have no place in a family
or community seeking to live together happily.

What about relationships in the workplace or in social
circles? Why do we make fun of others? There's a difference between joyful teasing and cutting sarcasm. Joyful
teasing can be healthy as long as it is lifting and not making light of another's tender feelings or sacred beliefs. Is it
possible to build self-esteem in others when we finally tire
of putting people down? Being critical of others seems to
create a self-inflicted fatigue that can only be relieved by
the renewing exercise of lifting people up.

A conscious effort to put people up rather than down
requires skills that must be nurtured with great care. For
example, we must learn to separate the behavior from the
individual, which requires time, patience, and maturity.
Most young people cannot accomplish this initially
because of their lack of experience. Most adults, however,
should be able to see that not all negative comments or
constructive criticism is meant to tear them down personally. Those we love we often chasten because of that love,
chastening that should be done in the spirit of lifting,
teaching, and building—not destroying. This can only be

done when genuine love exists, the love that enables us to separate an individual's negative behavior from their worth as individuals. Again, it is not easy for most of us to do. It requires an appreciation for and a belief in the significant nature of the individual and their boundless potential. Remember, we're trying to develop an art—the art of building others. It is work.

These chastisements or corrections have nothing to do with not liking or loving the individual disciplined. It is the art of being able to separate the person, who has endless worth, from the behaviors that are offensive.

As a teacher I occasionally have had to confront students who misbehaved and disrupted the learning of others. I try to help them understand that I love them as individuals but that some of their behaviors are unacceptable in a school setting. Sometimes, because of their youth, they think (and sometimes even express), "He just doesn't like me." Nothing could be further from the truth. In reality I love them and want them to be happy and successful in their lives, now and in the future. That's why it is essential that they learn which behaviors are not acceptable and will not be tolerated, for in the future, someone who perhaps doesn't love or care about them might cause them physical or emotional harm.

Suppose a child hits a baseball through the front room window. The last thing he or she needs to hear is, "You idiot! You just hit a ball through our front room window!" Rather, the child needs to be enfolded in loving arms and given guidance for a plan to repair the damage. Teenagers who make a foolish calculation and crunch the front end of dad's car do not a need a lecture on driving carefully but rather understanding fathers who know something about mistakes themselves. A dutiful wife who, while cleaning up her husband's mess on the bedroom dresser unknowingly throws away an important business paper, does not need a tirade from her husband; she needs help in trying to recover the paper. There is a difference between an honest mistake—something we humans are prone to—and the person who makes it. Of course young people need correction, but it must be done wisely. Can it not be done with persuasion, patience, gentleness, kindness, and unconditional love? Can we try and get all the information about a situation before coming to conclusions so that we're not viewed as hypocrites?

We must reprove as soon after the mistake has been made as possible, and then afterwards express our undeviating love so the one being reproved will not think of the reprover as his enemy. In short, he or she will be lifted and not feel put down and degraded.

Again, we must be builders and not destroyers. If we spent as much time lifting people up as we have in putting them down, think how effective we could be in building their self-esteem. Looking for honest ways to lift another would also be more beneficial to our own self-esteem, for we would see more good in ourselves. We would quit being so critical of our weaknesses and start finding ways to make our weaknesses become our strengths. Perhaps our outlook on life or on an uncomfortable circumstance would also be clearer.

2.

Help others to not fear failure, change, or success.

An entire chapter could be written about each of these three important elements; for now, let's just touch on them briefly. Sometimes people are so afraid of failure and of looking stupid in front of their peers that they never attempt anything new or creative. Their dreams often go unfulfilled. Their lives are less than they could be because they are too afraid to take a chance, to reach out and try new things. Realistically, failure is a common companion to all of us. Who among us has never made a mistake? We all do, with some regularity. And it's okay! I'm not saying we should get a Ph.D. in failure; I am simply saying that failing at something doesn't mean we are worthless. Because we perform badly at times does not equate with being a bad person. I don't know of anyone who has not failed at something, and generally we all fail numerous times. Failure is a part of life, and we should not fear it. Rather, our failures, if we let them, can be stepping-stones to a stronger character. Imagine how many times the ice skater has fallen before we appreciate her triple jumps or the gymnast has missed the bar before we see his flawless performance. Somehow we must help others understand— especially our children—that they will not always be victo- rious or come out on top in everything. There will always be those who are more talented. This is a reality of life. Let me illustrate with a story.

I'm acquainted with a teacher who, every workday for seven years, during the lunch hour, lost a ping-pong match to the same opponent. Now, losing at ping-pong may not seem like a big deal to most people, but the teacher who suffered defeat had an almost unconquerable competitive spirit. Getting crushed every day and having to listen to his fellow teacher-opponent talk about it for seven years was tough. Each day at lunch they would play one or two games. Each day at lunch he lost. With every loss he would remind the other player that these failures were mere stepping-stones to his eventual success. The other teacher, with an innocent mocking spirit, would then remind him that he could build the wall of China with all his stepping-stones! Quitting was never an option. In fact, he never once believed he would lose. He knew he was not a failure in life simply because of constant defeat in this one area, even if it did happen every day.

The day finally arrived when he became a fairly decent ping-pong player and could defeat his seven-year nemesis occasionally. Though failure was routine at first, his skills became better and better with time and practice. Life is like that: we can become better individuals, better fathers and husbands, wives and mothers, even better children, if we persist in reaching our goals. As the old saying goes, "That which we persist in doing becomes easier. Not that the nature of the task has changed, but our ability to do has increased." The concept of teaching others, and especially children, not to fear failure, is critical in building self-esteem.

Change is an interesting creature. It is frightening at times, but it is essential to our personal growth, and it plays an important part in the growth of families, communities, and organizations. We face it all the time. Change often causes us to stretch ourselves, and it forces us to leave our comfort zone. But is this stretching not the very process that so often brings us to our knees, humbling our hearts and providing opportunities for growth?

Change is an opportunity for growth; it is a strengthening process. Change is not to be feared, for surely it is the one thing in life on which we can count! Circumstances are always in a state of flux. When we learn to accept change without fearing it, something happens inside us. When we learn that the ability to make adjustments and to be flexible is a vital part of successful living, we feel better about ourselves and our circumstances.

It is strange but true: the fear of success is almost as frightening as the fear of failure. I remember watching an NCAA college basketball championship game on television one year. The coach of the underdog team was doing all he could to inspire his players to a victory. During a time-out he gathered his team around him. They were several points behind, and the situation did not look promising. The TV crew put their microphone near the huddle. As the coach talked, his players listened intently. His wisdom should always be remembered: "Gentlemen! Don't be afraid to win!" It was so simple, yet so profound. He sensed that they were afraid to win because very few expected it of them. They came from behind to eventually be victorious. When their fear of winning was eliminated, they put themselves in a position to succeed. As we teach ourselves, and our children, not to fear success, we allow ourselves to succeed at life. Success has a way of bringing opportunities for further growth, and if we can encourage people to keep success (and failure) in the proper perspective, their self-esteem will increase. We can do this by helping them view their successes for what they really are—opportunities to serve God and our fellow human beings.

If you are one who believes in God, is it not your belief that he wants you to succeed, and that he will help you to do so? However, it would be well for us to always remember to be grateful and appreciative to him for our success. May we teach all people this great lesson, to be grateful and to express gratitude. As an individual's life is filled with gratitude and thanksgiving their self-esteem cannot help but be enhanced. Then, failure, change, and success won't seem so frightening. Their self-esteem will increase as they allow these events to happen in their lives, and true growth will happen within them.

3.
Teach others to never fear the truth.

This is another way to build self-esteem. This point has been meaningful to me since I first heard in a movie some twenty five years ago the statement "Only if we are unafraid of truth will we ever find it." This statement sounds similar to what Jesus taught in the new testament: "You shall know the truth, and the truth shall make you free." The freedom to see ourselves as we really are can come to us if we do not fear the truth. Truth is hard on us because it requires us to admit that we are often wrong. It requires us to be humble, to eliminate pride from our lives, and to accept those things we cannot change. If we are afraid of truth our lives will be restricted. Fear affects how we view most things in our lives. As young and old alike learn to not fear the truth in any setting, they can learn to walk with confidence, knowing the road on which they travel is a safe one, and self-esteem is thus nurtured and strengthened. As the writer of 3 John voiced for all people who are builders of self-esteem, "I have no greater joy than to hear that my children walk in truth."

4.

Stop calling people names and labeling them
with damaging verbal barbs.

One of the worst forms of abuse, yet one we don't always notice in our own behavior, is to verbally tear down others. Why? Because "as he thinketh in his heart, so is he." We become what we think about most of the time—actions do grow out of our thoughts. How can people have their minds filled with positive, uplifting thoughts or care about people if they are constantly being called names that degrade or that damage their ability to see themselves for what they truly are and should be—kings and queens. How can their confidence wax strong if the individual hides within himself in order to escape the pain of verbal abuse? The answer is simple: It can't.

To build esteem in others, it would be helpful to keep in mind the following poem; written about children, it applies to people of all ages.

Children learn what they live and children live what they learn.

If children live with criticism, they learn to condemn.

If children live with tolerance, they learn to be patient.

If children live with ridicule, they learn to be shy.

But if children live with encouragement, they learn confidence.

If children live with security, they learn to have faith.

If children live with fear, they grow up standing at the end of every line.

But if children live with praise, they learn to stand alone and lead their parade even if it's raining.

If children are spoiled with indulgence and permissiveness, they grow up full of compromise and greed.

If children are given challenges and responsibilities, they grow up with values and goals.

If children live with depression, they'll need a drink, a puff, a sniff, a shot, a pill to get them high.

But if children live with optimism, they'll grow up thinking they were born to fly.

If children live with hate, they'll grow up blind to beauty and true love.

But if children live with love, they'll live to give their love away, and become blind to hate.

If children are reminded of all the bad in them we see, they'll become exactly what we hoped they'd never be.

But if we tell our children we're so proud to wear their name, they'll learn to win, believing they'll achieve their highest aim.

Because children live what they learn and children learn what they live.

(Denis Waitley, *2005: A Child's Odyssey* Rancho Santa Fe, Calif., 1982, [audio cassette])

5.

Talk to family members and others as you
would to a guest in your home.

This is closely related to no name-calling and is a vital step
in building others. The use of such simple phrases as
"please," " thank you," and "pardon me" make a world of difference in the way people feel about themselves and you.
How do you feel when someone speaks to you in angry or
rude tones? My grandmother used to tell me, "You can always catch more flies with honey than you can with vine-
gar." Or in other words, "A soft answer turneth away wrath:
but grievous words stir up anger."

An article given to me by a fellow teacher illustrates
this point with precision. Erma Bombeck is credited with
this humorous and thought-provoking anecdote.

On TV the other day, a leading child psychologist said
parents should treat their children as they would treat
their best friend . . . with courtesy,dignity, and diplomacy.

"I have never treated my children any other way," I told
myself. But later that night, I thought about it. Did I really
talk to my best friends like I talked to my children? Just
suppose . . . our good friends, Fred and Eleanor, came to
dinner one night and . . .

"Well, it's about time you two got here! What have you
been doing? Dawdling? Leave those shoes outside, Fred.
They've got mud on them. And shut the door. Were you
born in a barn?

"So, Eleanor, how have you been? I've been meaning to
have you over for such a long time. Fred! Take it easy on
the chip dip or you'll ruin your dinner. You all wash up and
I'll take up the food. Don't tell me your hands are clean,
Eleanor. I saw you playing with the dog.

"Fred, you sit over there, and Eleanor, you can sit with the half glass of milk. You know you're all elbows when it comes to milk. There now, your host will say grace.

"Fred, I don't see any cauliflower on your plate. Have you ever tried it? Well, try a spoonful. If you don't like it I won't make you finish it, but if you don't try it, you can just forget dessert. And sit up or your spine will grow that way. Now, what were we talking about? Oh yes, the Gerbers.

"They sold their house. I mean they took a beating but . . . Eleanor, don't talk with food in your mouth. I can't understand a word you're saying. And use your napkin."

At that moment in my fantasy, my son walked into the room. "How nice of you to come," I said pleasantly.

"Now what did I do," he sighed.

The way we talk to and treat people can indeed make a difference in how they feel about themselves.

6.

Help others learn to accept a compliment.

This is such a simple concept that most people haven't given it much thought, but how people accept a compliment shows a great deal about how they feel toward themselves. Two simple words are sufficient when someone compliments us: "thank you"; "you're kind" or "thank you very much" are also acceptable. Feigning modesty or denying that the compliment is true is counterproductive.

For some reason we often feel that we need to put ourselves down in order to be built up. Even if we don't believe the compliment to be true, a simple "thank you" expresses appreciation. It is amazing what happens. By simply saying "thank you," the individual sends a positive message to herself that she is okay instead of concentrating on her frailties or suspicions of others' hidden agendas. One of the truly great tragedies of our time is that so many people seem to be so ungrateful. Let us not be guilty of this but rather be grateful for the little things and say a simple thank-you when someone gives us a compliment. May we also learn that when someone truly deserves to be complimented we should do all we can to lift their self-esteem by giving them the opportunity to show their gratitude and say thank you. When others learn this simple concept, they can learn to be gracious as they enhance their self-esteem.

7.
Teach others to be the best they can be.

If people are going to feel secure about themselves and have deep inner strength, they must be taught to be the best they can be, which may not be the best in the world. Just do the best you can do! We do all we can do and then rely on the grace of God for the outcome.

Obviously, some people can do more than others. If we always compare our accomplishments with others' achievements and abilities, we will end up being disappointed for much of our lives. There will always be someone who is a little better, a little faster, a little smarter, a little stronger, or a little bigger than we are. This should not throw us, however, or cause us to lose confidence in our own strengths and talents. It simply means that we are individuals, with our own unique set of strong points. Perhaps this is why those who possess the attribute of true charity—no matter what situation they are in or who they are with or how they perform—are not jealous, proud, or selfish. They appear to have learned the lesson that it is what we are deep down inside that matters and not the outward appearance.

Some years ago I had a student who taught me more about this concept than I ever taught him in school. His name was David. I have no way of knowing why his parents named him David, but no one ever had a more fitting name. Many are familiar with the biblical story of the young shepherd boy David killing Goliath, the Philistine giant. My student David was born with a Goliath that by most standards would not have allowed him to accomplish anything—he was born with no arms, with only short deformed limbs protruding from each shoulder. The only thing that his handicap prevented him from doing was taking care of some of his personal needs. However, even these needs were doable with an ingenious invention that allowed him to function almost normally most of the time. Other than that, nothing stopped him. Possessing a brilliant mind that he used to lift others with quick wit and humor, he was a student leader at the high school. He played the cornet in the marching band. He serves faithfully in his church and community and is currently enrolled in college. David does the best he can do, given his set of circumstances. Obviously he will never play quarterback in the NFL or be a goalie in the NHL. But if you want to learn about life and how to be successful at living, and doing the best you can do, you will be hard-pressed to find a greater teacher.

8.

Recognize that abnormal or unruly behavior is often
a cry for help or a sign of insecurity.

Many times a child or young person (and at times adults), may reject the very help they need because they do not realize how desperately they need it; in such cases we cannot stop trying to help. We need to be aware that the problem usually runs deeper than it appears on the surface.

At times it can be very discouraging to be a teacher. The desire to help, teach, and inspire students is great, but occasionally the student doesn't want to be helped. Usually such an individual is struggling personally, and his or her seemingly unbridled behavior is a cry for help. While I'm not a psychologist, I've seen this situation many times.

I remember a young man who I thought hated me and my children; I had no idea what I'd done to warrant his wrath. One day I asked him what was troubling him, and I was shocked at his response. Everything he said cannot be written because it would not be appropriate to print, but the gist of it was that, in his mind, we had everything he desired: a happy family with a dad and mom at home, where peace was common. His anger toward me and my family came from an inner pain. Once we talked and cleared the air and he felt that I understood, things began to change.

One day he came to my office and asked if we could talk. His eyes filled with tears as he asked, in his childlike naivete if it was possible for me to forgive him for having been disrespectful to me. He honestly thought he was going to hell for swearing at me and manifesting such a hatred for me and my family. As he began to mature and better understand life and as he overcame his anger at not having what he desired, his behavior improved and we became quite close friends. When problems are cleared, many times the undesirable behavior is eliminated and self-esteem improves.

9.
Help children develop a sense of belonging.

It sounds simple, but this is a difficult task in the art of building self-esteem in others. When people feel accepted, wanted, needed, loved, and a part of things, there is life. They feel worthwhile, and there is an inner calm and glow about them because their basic need for approval is met. On the other hand, when they don't have this need satisfied, something inside them is stunted or dies, and often negative thoughts and feelings grow to maturity.

Most individuals want desperately to be loved by those close to them, especially other family members and peers. Again, it seems so simple. But why do so many people feel lonely, unwanted, unimportant? Why are so many people engaged in self-destructive behaviors? From my observation it is the greatest feeling in the world to be loved and to have a sense of belonging.

Realizing that there are exceptions—some children don't feel close to their parents—why do so many children love their parents so deeply? Is it because the parents first loved the children? Words cannot express how a young man or woman must feel when they look up into the stands at a ball-game or into the audience at a concert, play, or recital and see their number-one fans: their parents. When they sense that their parents love them it really doesn't matter how they perform; they know they are loved and that they belong to a family unit. They know they're wanted at home. They know there will be love and acceptance waiting for them. With this type of belonging, how could they feel anything but good about themselves? After all, it isn't the game, or the play, concert, or recital that matters. It is them! Please send love messages to your children so that they are not starved for affection and acceptance. It appears that it is often hard for fathers to put their arms around their sons and daughters, but it is absolutely crucial if they want to develop relationships that will meet the needs their children have for Dad's love and approval.

If we can generate in people a desire to help others' sense of belonging and being loved, they will begin to feel it themselves. Why? Because the vision of who they are and where they fit in will be seared into their souls, and they will know and feel that they belong. If we belong nowhere else, we all belong to the family of God.

10.
Recognize the difference between adolescence and an adolescent.

Adolescence is a very difficult time in life through which we all pass; an adolescent, on the other hand, is a thinking, feeling human being who is going through a sometimes difficult stage of development. When we understand this concept we can become builders instead of destroyers. When we are empathetic to the challenges faced (growing pains, blemished skin, burgeoning relationships, physical awkwardness, and raging hormones), we will be more lov-

76

ing and appreciative of adolescents' struggles and thus be solid friends and confidantes, laying a foundation for them to move out into the world with the confidence to deal with others. They know that they always have a home base to return to when the world treats them cruelly.

If you have one or more teenagers in the home, you have learned, or will learn, that it can be quite an emotional roller coaster! In fact, you will learn how hard it is, at times, to practice what you preach. You may find your spouse continually reminding you that it wasn't that long ago that you were going through the same sensitive time in life. You may even be told you have a short memory! It is not always helpful to a young person to be reminded of the principle that when hormones run wild, the brain seems to shut down. We remember how it felt when it seemed that no one understood. We would do well to remember how unsure we were about so many things as we passed through adolescence. It is a difficult time for many, but an adolescent is a human being with sensitive feelings and usually rather fragile self-esteem. If we're going to be true builders it is essential that we clearly see that distinction. Again, the educator Neal A. Maxwell has taught that "In the healthy family, first and best, we can learn to listen, forgive, praise, and to rejoice in the achievements of others. There also we can learn to tame our egos, work, repent, and love. In families with spiritual perspective, yesterday need not hold tomorrow hostage. If we sometimes act the fool, loving families know this is not our last act; the curtain is not run down."

11.

Make a valiant effort to learn and use people's names.

There is nothing so beautiful as the sound of your own name, even if you don't particularly like it! Isn't it heart-warming to have someone call you by name after a long period of separation? You experience feelings of worth when you realize that time and distance have not dulled their memory of you. On the other hand, when parents try to get a specific child's attention, they often go through the entire list of their children's names—including the dog's—before they settle upon the correct one. Though this common, human, and sometimes comical situation may not be damaging to an individual's self-esteem, it sometimes can cause a young person to feel frustration and possibly wonder if we recognize that they are individuals rather than just part of the group. This is such a simple act. Can we not each strive to learn and use each others' names?

12.

Help others live good, honest, moral lives.

Every year, for many years, Cecil B. DeMille's classic film *The Ten Commandments,* starring Charlton Heston, is viewed by millions.

We keep watching it but perhaps do not understand how significant the Ten Commandments really are. For many, this film is the only association they have with the word "commandment." If we only catch glimpses of the movie and we never study religious writings, it is easy to be lulled into the thought pattern that God only gave ten suggestions to Moses rather than ten commandments. *The American Heritage Dictionary of the English Language* defines the word commandment as: 1. A command; edict. 2. Often commandment. Any of the Ten Commandments.

Could going back to the basic, old-fashioned, Christian values of keeping the commandments of God be a vital step in building self-esteem? Whether you have a specific religious persuasion or even if you do not believe in God, there are principles, that if lived produce peaceful, happy lives. Just being good, moral, and striving to help others do the same is the best way I know to recognize our true nature and care about others. Again, as we help others do this, it happens within ourselves.

There is a direct relationship between our ability to follow these commandments and our ability to love, not only others and deity, but also ourselves. If we love goodness, try to do what we believe is right, care more about our values and principles than what others think of us, with all my heart I believe we will have self-esteem. If we fail at everything else, let us not fail at loving our children and others so that they will experience us as builders rather than destroyers. Just help people, and especially youth, to understand that there is nothing bad about being as good as they want to be.

Chapter Seven

The Power of Spirituality

T he very word "spirituality" conjures up a wide range of feelings, attitudes, opinions, and responses, depending on an individual's upbringing, religious preference or non-preference, daily experience, and lifestyle. It seems that spirituality has become a lost art. People are afraid of offending others. It appears that many are afraid to talk about spiritual matters in mixed circles. I see it as more than an art—it is a gift or talent that must be developed. In fact, to me, it is the greatest of all the talents and gifts that one can acquire because when life ends and our bodies are laid to rest in the cold earth, spirituality is the only thing we carry with us. It's obvious that none of us get out of this earthly experience alive. We will all die. As that day approaches—or comes suddenly for some—what really matters? Other than relationships with loved ones and deity, what else is there? Are worldly possessions important when a child lies dying in a hospital bed after a tragic accident? When a natural disaster destroys everything, is the first thing we look for our car, or our family members? Again, what matters when the pressure is really on? What you know and what you feel is all that goes with us when life ends.

Why are we afraid of developing spiritual talents along with the mental, emotional, physical, and social? Spirituality helps individuals understand their feelings. If human beings become past feeling, we are in trouble as individuals, families, nations, businesses and citizens of the world. We must be able to feel or we become just advanced animals that don't care about one another. Our feelings begin to wax cold. Love, caring and compassion for one another is lost. As the old saying goes, we are not human beings trying to have a spiritual experience—we are spiritual beings trying to have a human experience.

The prolific writer and thinker C. S. Lewis made this perceptive observation.

> It is a serious thing to live in a society of possible gods and goddesses, to remember that the dullest and most uninteresting person you can talk to may one day be a creature which, if you saw it now, you would be strongly tempted to worship, or else a horror and a corruption such as you now meet, if at all, only in a nightmare. All day long we are, in some degree, helping each other to one or other of these destinations. It is in the light of these overwhelming possibilities, it is with the awe and the circumspection proper to them, that we should conduct all our dealings with one another, all friendships, all loves, all play, all politics. There are no *ordinary* people. You have never talked to a mere mortal. Nations, cultures, arts, civilizations—these are mortal, and their life is to ours as the life of a gnat. But it is immortals whom we joke with, work with, marry, snub, and exploit—immortal horrors or everlasting splendors.
>
> (*The Weight of Glory and Other Addresses* [New York: Macmillan Publishing Company, 1980], pp. 18,19.)

Something happens in a person when he or she finally realizes—realizes deep in the soul—that each individual is of value and that every living human being has some of the divine within him or her. This makes people and behaviors change. Once we accept that each individual is more than a physical or mental being, that realization changes us, and our desire to willingly injure others or transgress against them leaves. Our lives then begin to be governed by moral principles and values. Morality is not something to be hidden and swept under the carpet. We begin to understand the value of law and order and that the most meaningful laws in a society are moral laws. It is morally wrong to kill, to rape, to steal, to abuse, to lie, to be unfaithful to a spouse and/or children. These simple, profound beliefs have a very practical value. They bring a feeling of dignity, of self-respect. Self-pity and depression begin to fade away. We then can yield to self-discipline and the discipline of living a morally strong life and accept even the very hard lessons. This understanding is spirituality.

If ever there were a time in which the power to live by moral and correct principles was needed, it is now. A blanket of darkness and gloom seems to be covering the earth as never before. But it can be overcome.

Corruption is rapidly expanding in every segment of our society. It is more highly organized, more cleverly disguised, and more powerfully promoted than ever before. Gangs, drug cartels and secret organizations lusting for power, gain, and glory are flourishing. Some organizations even seek to overthrow the freedom of all lands, nations, and countries. Their evil influence appears to be ever on the rise.

On the other hand, goodness is also on the rise! The numbers of those who desire to be and do good is growing. Light can overcome darkness. Hopefully we can learn from the past and not become like so many other societies that fell into spiritual decline and eventually self-destructed.

With the power of negative influences increasing and as they become ever more organized, it is vital that we see things clearly. We must see things as they really are, and as they really will be. Without the power of spirituality or the ability to feel, it is impossible to see ourselves and our future with such clarity. But remember, spirituality is not acquired suddenly. It is the consequence of a succession of good choices. It is the harvest of living a good life based on sound and correct principles and values.

If ever there were a time when youth (as well as adults,) needed to stand tall, be brave, and stay true to their principles and values, it is now. Consider some statistics: In 1987 the American Medical Association reported that the three major killers of youth between the ages of fifteen and twenty-four were in order: accidents (60 percent of those were auto accidents, and often those auto accidents were drug-or alcohol-related), homicide, and suicide. The statistics have not changed much in the past decade. At the time of this writing AIDS has crept in as a major killer along with the three previously mentioned. With drug-and alcohol-related car accidents, murder, suicide, and AIDS heading the list as the leading killers of teenagers, do all of us need to be brave and fight the scourge that seems to be engulfing us? The answer is obvious. But such bravery requires great effort. This kind of moral courage will not destroy an individual's credibility—it will surely enhance it. When an individual acts in harmony with his or her own conscience and beliefs, he or she has fulfilled the fundamental requirement for inner peace and security.

Four of the most significant ways of getting and maintaining the vision that comes through spirituality are four of the same principles most people have been taught from their youth. They are: first, prayer or meditation; second, the study of religious writings and or Scripture, and listening to or reading books and tapes that teach values and successful living; third, running from anything that would destroy peace and happiness or harm others; and fourth, service to others.

1.

Prayer or meditation.

As children, many of us sat in Sunday School or other religious services and learned of the importance of prayer. What has happened to our ability to believe and our child-like faith and acceptance of a power greater than ourselves? Have we become so sophisticated that we think we can maneuver the stormy seas of life all alone without help from above? As we strive to be good, the power of spirituality brings us back to our roots and to the simple things in life. I'm not talking about just saying prayers to say words or meditating because we don't have anything else to do. I'm talking about truly giving thanks and being grateful, and pleading for divine guidance, asking for forgiveness, strength, courage, charity, endurance, and so on.

To illustrate this point I share a brief story and a poem that has brought me often to my knees. One night after I gave a lecture a man approached me and handed me a poem. He told me the story of the poem's author, of whom I had read in the local newspaper for years. The author of the poem had been convicted of molesting and murdering several young boys, and he was sentenced to die by lethal injection. A few days before the execution the man who gave me the poem was called to the prison for his final visit.

During that visit the prisoner asked the man (who served as the his religious advisor) to please share the poem with the youth of America in hopes that they wouldn't end up in a similar situation. The man then said to me, "Please, when the time is right, will you publish this poem and speak about it whenever you feel you can in order to help me carry out the author's request and to teach people the importance of prayer, regardless of their religious affiliations or beliefs?" Hopefully, by sharing this poem every reader will be helped and the author will have some peace. The poem is entitled "The Wrong Path Chosen."

> I wonder where I went wrong,
> In my youth and in my past.
> Life's changes were quite sudden
> To bring good to bad so fast.
>
> In eagerness I started out,
> Life's mysteries to explore.
> My parents gave me a good life.
> In foolishness I sought more.
>
> My youth held some accomplishments,
> Great was my hope to please.
> My desires to serve the Lord
> Brought me often to my knees.
>
> Upon my path temptation came
> Which alone, I couldn't escape.
> Too proud to call for needed help,
> I chose my dreadful fate.

My future now holds little hope
And my life is full of fear.
The sentence of death upon me
Calls hell's presence oh so near.

Deep within these prison walls
I'll spend the rest of life.
No more dreams or hopes or pleasures.
Never to have my own family or wife.

The nights are getting longer,
The days . . . yet longer still.
I need to find some inner strength
To climb my last big hill.

I pray it's not too late for me.
To purge my soul from sin,
Or remove the doubt within my heart
So Heaven may let me in.

To young people I would say,
Be true! Be just! Be fair!
Follow the teachings of the Lord,
And fill your days with prayer.

No matter what our religious affiliation, this poem is very thought-provoking. We each need extra help at times in our lives and should not feel hesitant to seek out our God and ask for needed strength.

2.

The study of religious writings and or Scripture,
and listening to or reading books and tapes
that teach values and successful living.

Throughout history the old axiom has proved to be true that "the pen is mightier than the sword."

I do a lot of traveling and speaking, and I dislike hotel rooms. But the one advantage to being alone in a hotel room is that I can take a shower as long and hot as I desire. Having a wife and four daughters it is often very difficult to get a long or hot shower at home. So when I'm traveling, I take full advantage. The relaxing water drenches me. The hot showers drenching our bodies can be likened to the liberating and exhilarating experience of searching and studying the words of others which can give life and vision and spiritual strength. The Psalmist wrote, "How sweet are thy words unto my taste! yea, sweeter than honey to my mouth! . . .Thy word is a lamp unto my feet, and a light unto my path."

Has studying and learning become sweet to our taste and like honey to our mouths? Does what we learn and study guide our decision-making processes? Do we have a reservoir of knowledge and/or spiritual understanding that is deep enough for us to be self-reliant and self-sufficient so that we're not blown in every direction as a wave upon the sea when the storms of life beat down upon us? Have we become familiar enough with the words and teachings we have available to us so that we become, as Mr. Keating tried to teach his students in the movie *Dead Poets Society,* able to allow the words of the poets and "prophets" to ooze from our lips like honey? As we open the pages of Scripture, history, and literature do the writers speak to us? Do we hear them? Do we feel them? Do they become a part of us? Or are they just words on a page that greet blind eyes and fall upon deaf ears and ricochet off hardened hearts?

One of the great teachers in my life once stated, "I find that when we get casual in our relationships with divinity and we feel that we are alone or that no divine ear is listening, when we feel far, far away from our spiritual roots, if we will immerse ourselves in Scriptures and other uplifting literature, the distance can narrow and spirituality can return. We can then find ourselves loving more intensely those whom we must love and loving them more as well as being more kind and gentle and tolerant." But to immerse ourselves is more than mere dipping: it requires time, work, effort, pondering, or meditation.

As technology continues to increase at lightning speed we must not forget the basics. By just doing the simple things we stay close to our spiritual roots.

3.
Running from anything that would destroy peace and happiness or harm others.

In order to maintain a high level of spiritual sensitivity we must learn to run from any temptation or situation that would destroy our inner peace and be contrary to our moral values. (This topic will be covered at length in Chapter Nine.)

4.

Service to others.

One of the best and most clear indicators that we are pro-gressing and becoming spiritually sensitive is the way we treat other people. Rendering service not only helps others but takes our minds off ourselves, which allows us to put our problems in perspective. Getting our minds off our-selves, serving others, and working to relieve human suf-fering not only brings a sense of spiritual power into our lives but is what life really is all about. Be one who nurtures and who builds. Be one who has an understanding and a forgiving heart, who looks for the best in people. By serving people we leave them better than we found them. By serv-ing we become fair with our competitors, whether in busi-ness, athletics, or elsewhere. By caring about others and seeking to meet their needs, we don't get drawn into the seemingly dominant attitude of our times—trying to win by intimidation or by undermining someone's character. Lend a hand to those who are frightened, lonely, or burdened.

If we could look into others' hearts and understand the unique challenges each of us faces, hopefully we would treat each other much more gently, with more love, patience, tolerance, and care.

Isn't the essence of spirituality serving others? Does not the service of others equate with serving God? The power of spirituality which comes from being good is personified by serving others. Serving people is so important because people matter more than anything—possessions, honors, power, careers, or educational degrees. Perhaps a story can best illustrate my point.

As a young boy I dreamed of owning a Schwinn three-speed bike with the gears mounted on the handlebars just above the sparkling red-plastic handle grips. The bike I wanted had long, thin, plastic streamers hanging from the handle grips, of various colors: red, yellow, white, green, and blue. And they had a distinct smell—just like a new Christmas doll. The bike had a two-tone red-and-white seat with a large white S in the middle and skinny tires. Hand brakes are common today, but back then they were new. I had never ridden a bike with hand brakes, and I longed to do so.

For years each Christmas brought the hope that somehow my parents could afford my dream bike. That hope never materialized. It seemed as if I always received the same things: an orange and hardtack candy in my stocking, some underwear (I wanted boxer shorts but usually got briefs with red dots around the waistband!), socks, and a pair of Levis with a button fly. Here again, my desire was for something different: I wanted a zipper, for buttons weren't really in style then. I also usually received some T-shirts, a basketball, and once in a while, some pajamas.

Many Christmas mornings found me disappointed because I didn't receive what I wanted. At the time, I never realized how hard my parents had worked and how much they had sacrificed to provide what they could.

Christmas changed for me years later when I was a grown man. One evening as I drove home from work a public service announcement from the state social services agency came on the radio. They were asking for volunteers to provide Christmas gifts for those patients at the state hospital who had no family or friends. What a great idea! When I arrived home I ran into the house and presented the proposal to my wife. She listened patiently and then told me I was too late—she had heard the same announcement and had already called the hospital to have a patient assigned to us. We were both thrilled to have this opportunity to buy for a needy person instead of just for ourselves and our own children.

The gentleman was fifty-five years of age. He suffered from severe mood disorders and just needed a few items of clothing wrapped in decorative paper. After reading the list of what he needed, I stood in the kitchen in disbelief. For the most part, the only things he needed were the very things I had hated as a young boy: T-shirts, underwear, socks, and pajamas. It was unbelievable! Rarely in my life had I felt more humbled. It seemed that I was being given the opportunity to make up, somewhat, for all my ingratitude as a child.

The hospital gave us strict orders not to bring food items or extra gifts. I thought, however, that a couple of nice dress shirts surely couldn't hurt, so I bought them, wrapped them, and put them with the rest of our patient's packages.

The day arrived for taking the gifts to the hospital. Our children got in the car with my wife, Melanie, and me, and we made our way downtown on snowy roads. When we arrived we were directed to the lock down facility, which caused a little apprehension in us. I went to the steps, rang the bell, and waited for someone to open the iron-barred door; it wasn't long before a young orderly answered it. I stated my business, gave him the patient's name, and handed him the packages. He told me that our patient was having a good day and then asked if I would like to bring my entire family inside so we could give him the gifts ourselves. We were led to a small dining area and our patient, who was in a wheelchair, was brought out to meet us.

He had a blanket wrapped around his legs and was wearing a sweatshirt. His face was covered with a two- or three-days growth of beard, and crumbs from his dinner were spread all around his mouth. He could not, or would not, speak.

The orderly asked him if he wanted to open the packages or if he wanted the Christiansons to do it. No response. The orderly handed us the packages and we began opening them one by one. As we did so, tears began streaming down the patient's cheeks. One of our young daughters started to cry and asked, "Doesn't he like our presents? Is he sad that we brought him pajamas?"

We tried to explain that they were tears of joy, but she was too young to understand. I was flabbergasted. Here was this sweet, lonely man crying over T-shirts, pajamas, socks, and underwear with red dots around the waist-band—the very items I had once scoffed at. Humility swept over me like a cold sweat. There was no need to speak— we just felt deep gratitude for the blessing of giving.

As we drove home, the car was silent. We each had been deeply moved. However, when we pulled into the driveway my daughter again said she still didn't understand why the man cried if he was happy. Again, we tried to explain, but more importantly, we tried to teach our children about the joy of giving. Serving others took on new meaning for our family.

We never saw that man again, and the programs at the hospital have changed over the years, but we have tried to do something special for others ever since. We have all been changed as a result. Christmas is now the most exciting time of the year for all of us. We can hardly wait to give and bless others' lives. Of course, we should be giving, blessing, and serving every day, but doing it at Christmas has a special significance. The joy I feel when serving means much more than any possession I own or desire to have.

Truly, spirituality and the ability to feel and be sensitive to others is a power that comes from being good. It is a power from which everyone on earth could benefit. If we all cared about each other a little more and tried a little harder to be good the entire world would be a happier place and there would be less sorrow and more joy.

Seeking spirituality is not something to be feared or to shy away from. As we strive to obtain it, our lives will be more fulfilled and our hearts will gain desired peace. Hopefully, as we strive to incorporate into our lives the four practices suggested in this chapter we will understand and know that spirituality is a vital link to all who want happiness and true freedom.

Chapter Eight

The Power of Happiness and Freedom

Many years ago, as a young teacher of high school students I had an exceptional experience with a group of high school seniors. I left the classroom that day motivated to continue teaching and with the exhilarating feeling of walking on air. The class session had been far more than I had hoped it would when preparing the lesson, and it appeared that each student, or at least most students, had a great learning experience and left the class desiring to learn more. Several students thanked me for the class as they departed. I made my way to the office hoping to enjoy the sweetness of the moment a little longer.

Upon entering the office I noticed a folded three-by-five card was lying on the floor. Someone had evidently slipped it under the door after the class. In my pride I thought: "Wow! Someone enjoyed the class so much they had to write me a note about it!"

But after reading the neatly printed poem on the inside of the card, my heart sank as if to the gutter. The note read:

> Every human being is trying to say
> Something to others,
> Trying to cry out,
> I am alive,
> Notice me,
> Speak to me,
> Listen to me,

Confirm to me that I am
Important!
That I matter.
"God bless us with a listening ear."

I sat at my desk stunned, humbled beyond words. I pondered and cried. Amidst all my pride, at least one student felt unloved, unimportant, and ignored. Thoughts of the teacher training movie *Cipher in the Snow* raced through my mind. The movie tells the true story of the death of a young student who was virtually unknown by any other students or teachers. He dies in a snow bank after asking his bus driver to stop and let him off the bus. The investigation of his death proved he did not die of illness, but of a broken heart caused by loneliness and neglect. Could this same scenario actually be happening in my classroom? Such things only happened to others, or in the movies.

For nearly three years I searched in vain for the identity of the student who had written the note. Nothing. No one admitted to writing it.

Then, almost three years later, early one morning, about 3 or 4 a.m., a knock came at my door. I put on my robe, walked to the door, and asked who it was. When I opened the door, a former student of mine, reeking of alcohol, fell into my arms, sobbing.

I helped him into the living room and called for my wife to help me. He continued to sob; speaking words I couldn't understand. We found out he had been to a party where drugs and alcohol were being abused very freely, and there was also Satan-worship being practiced. He told us he was so scared that he came to a place where he knew he would be safe. Eventually he finally calmed down.

For some reason I asked him if he had written the poem on the three-by-five card. He said: "It's about time you figured it out. I thought you never would."

"Why did you write it?" I asked. "Did you really feel you were unimportant?"

"All you ever cared about were the athletes and the cheerleaders," he replied. "You never really showed much attention to the rest of us."

I asked him, "Well, then why are you here? Why did you come to me for help if you felt I didn't care?"

I don't remember how he responded, but I do know I hugged him and expressed my love for him. He stayed for a few hours, slept a little, and freshened up before returning to his apartment.

Now, many years later, he is doing quite well. We still see one another occasionally and we love each other dearly. That experience changed me. The agony and sorrow I felt, sitting at my desk, thinking that someone in my class was hurting and I wasn't helping them in their time of need—this haunted me. I am a different man today and hopefully a better teacher.

This—and similar experiences—helped me form a teaching philosophy based on the value of individuals and their desire to be happy. So far, it has been very successful. This philosophy has evolved as I have grown through experience and have tried to better understand that everyone does matter and that all need to know they are important.

Each new school year begins with this simple quote by Henry David Thoreau in mind: "I have never met a man [or woman] who is not my superior in at least one way." My philosophy is that because every human being is superior to me in at least one way—and often in many ways—they should be respected, regardless of their age, as worthwhile, significant individuals. As a teacher I want to contribute to the happiness of my students, as well as to the happiness of my family and others around me.

If life really has a purpose, then there must be more to life than simply existing to live and then to die. Are you happy? Do you agree that every human being is trying to say something to others? Are many trying to cry out to have their worth confirmed? Do we have listening ears? Are you happy? Are you at peace with how you live your life? Take one minute to reflect in silence on your inner feelings. In your heart of hearts, what are you really? What occupies your thoughts and your time? Again, are you happy and at peace? Are you free? Isn't that what most human beings spend their time, energy, and money striving for? Have all the troubles, tragedies, heartache, and sorrow that surround us every day, caused us to lose focus on all the good things in life? Have we lost sight of all the blessings we have even though all of us experience difficulties and great challenges? Happiness ought to be the object and design of our existence. It can be and will be if we pursue the path that leads to it. What is this path? It is uprightness and faithfulness to moral values and principles: it is being good! This happiness, this joy in daily living, this peace of conscience—these are some of the great powers that come from being good.

If one of the major desires and purposes of our lives on earth is to be happy and filled with joy, why then are there so many unhappy people? Why are so many downtrodden and browbeaten? Why have so many lost hope?

Perhaps all these questions cannot be answered. In fact, I'm not sure there are answers to some of them. But this much I do know: there is a direct relationship between our striving to be good and our ability to be happy and joyful.

Several times in the past when I've spoken about this subject, people have come up to me and voiced their frustration. They say, "I'm a good person who is trying to do everything I can that I believe is right, and I still feel miserable and unhappy most of the time. I don't like myself. I don't enjoy life. What you are saying just isn't true!"

Again, there may not be answers for all of life's difficult questions and problems. I also realize that some physical disorders (such as chemical imbalances) and emotional or mental disorders may be major factors in our behavioral patterns. But let's consider a couple of items.

The reality of being human is that bad things sometimes happen to good people. Doing everything we can to live according to our moral values does not mean we will be free of tragedy. One of the great lessons in life is learning that there is opposition in everything. It exists even when things are going great . . . especially when things are going great. Opposition is actually a wise and exacting teacher if we are wise enough to learn from it rather than becoming bitter and giving up on life. We cannot know happiness and joy if we do not know heartache and sorrow.

Life consists of many experiences; some are not only unfortunate, but completely unfair. Tragedies happen in all of our lives, and we all struggle from time to time. One key to success lies in how we deal with these situations. Some setbacks come as a result of our poor choices, while others come as a result of the poor choices of others. You may simply be a victim of someone else's misuse of his or her agency. Some setbacks come because we have imperfect bodies and we live in an imperfect world.

M. Scott Peck began his best-selling book *The Road Less Traveled* by writing "Life is difficult. This is a great truth, one of the greatest truths. It is a great truth because once we truly see this truth, we transcend it. Once we truly understand and accept it—then life is no longer difficult. Because once it is accepted, the fact that life is difficult no longer matters."

When will we come to learn that happiness and peace do not always equate with everything in life running smoothly and being unruffled? Happiness, joy, peace and freedom are powers that come from within as we continue to live by true and virtuous principles even amidst adversity.

If we continue to be good through difficult times we learn that God uses broken things to teach us some of life's greatest lessons. Remember: "It takes broken soil to produce a crop, broken clouds to give rain, broken bread to give strength. It is the broken alabaster box that gives forth perfume. . . . it is Peter, weeping bitterly, who returns to greater power than ever." (Vance Havner quoted in *Guidepost* (Oct. 1981), pg. 5.)

Consider the "Wayfarers Lament," written by my teaching colleague and friend John Young.

"O' Lord, I was caught up in the raging flood,
    wrenched from my path and purpose, and
    nearly drowned time and time again.

"I was dashed from stone to stone with merciless force,
    choked with water and tossed this way and that.

"In pain and terror I wept for my helplessness, my
    weakness, and called upon thee for help. I
    poured out my soul with all the energy I
    possessed for help, but where wast thou?

"I was bruised and broken and dragged for miles in the current. Unable to escape the force of the stream. I was battered until I had no will left even to live. I put my destiny in thine hand, and where wast thou?

"The terrors of the tide drove from me all care for the things of my life; my possessions; my place among men; and in the end, even care for my life itself.

"All strength to resist was taken from me, all energy to strive against the waves. And then, when I was weakened beyond pride, beyond fear, beyond care for anything, and I simply yielded myself to the flow, I found myself limp, and breathless on this foreign shore.

"O' Lord, where wast thou?"

"My son: Thou hast traveled far, through grief, toil, and trial. Thou standest here naked—dispossessed of all things and all earthly cares. Thou standest here on sacred ground, in a new and promised land.

"My son, I was always with thee.

"I was the water!"

Are the waters of life taking you to and fro and beating you against the rocky shores? Are their currents strong and powerful? Does it seem that it is impossible to change or to be happy and free because you've tried before and failed? You've been this way for so long and previous attempts to change have been unsuccessful, so why try? But everyone can be happy no matter how much sorrow, heartache, disappointment, or failure have been brought into their lives by the currents of life's teaching waters. What we need is to live by true and correct principles, realize that life is work and is difficult, and let the power of being good work its miracle. We must be brave as the current moves us, and that bravery comes by living the principles we discussed in the last chapter. We must be brave! We must!

Some years ago I heard a college president tell the story of his father, who was dying of bone cancer. He said that his father's condition became so bad that he had to be hospitalized and under constant supervision. Members of the family took turns sitting with their father and grandfather. They met his various needs and tried to make his last remaining days as pleasant as possible for someone with such a painful disease, for as the cancer eats away the life of the body, it causes the bones to become brittle, causing excruciating and almost unbearable pain. Such was the case with this man's father.

One night while the president sat with the dying man, his father gingerly crawled out of bed and knelt on the floor to pray. Instantly, the son reached down and tried to help his father back up into bed. The father refused to be helped. The son asked what he was doing and the father replied that he needed to pray. He said he had a very important question to ask God that required him to kneel. The son responded that in light of his condition he was sure that God would hear and answer prayers just as well if he were on his back, in bed, as he would if he were on his knees. Again the father refused. He said he must kneel. Again the son tried in vain to persuade him that it was okay to pray from bed, considering the circumstances. The father continued to refuse. Just the act of getting out of bed and kneeling could have caused bones to fracture, as well as other complications, but the father continued to insist that his question was so serious that it required kneeling. Finally the son asked what was so important that he just couldn't pray from bed. The father's response was sobering.

He said: "Son, I want to know why when I have been good all my life; why, when I have done what I believed was right and true every day of my life; why, when I have lived my religion every day, and been faithful to my family, and been honest in all my dealings with everyone; why, as this life comes to an end—why is God allowing me to suffer so miserably?" The son was shocked and stunned. He had nothing to say. He simply said, "Dad, I guess you had better pray from your knees." What would you say to such a question? How would you respond? It's a tough one, isn't it? Why do people who try so hard to do what is right end up suffering as much, and sometimes more, than those who just live for the day and do as they please, never worrying about anyone other than themselves? Perhaps the father's reply can give us some insight in to such difficult questions.

After praying, the father, with the help of his college-president son, got back into bed and the conversation continued. The son asked if his father had received the answer he had sought. The father was somewhat reluctant to give a reply, but with a bit more prodding he finally said: "Yes, son, I did get an answer. I learned that God needs brave sons, and I must learn to be brave!"

What a profound lesson to learn about being happy and free. We must be brave! God needs brave sons and he needs brave daughters and we must be brave. Very few statements have had as much affect on my attitude and outlook on life than the thought that God needs brave sons and he needs brave daughters and I must learn to be brave, no matter how hard life may be or what I may have to go through to learn the lessons.

Instead of asking the question "Why me?" when something terrible happens in our lives, why don't we have the bravery and courage to ask such questions as, "What can I learn from this?" or, "How can I use this experience to help others?" All difficult things will give us experience and will be for our good, if we do not weaken. No suffering or pain or heartache is ever wasted if we believe that we are to be happy and free. Suffering intensifies our education; it enhances the development of qualities such as patience, faith, fortitude, and humility. As previously mentioned, all that we suffer and endure—especially when we endure it patiently—not only gives us experience, but it builds our characters and makes us more tender and charitable towards others. It is through sorrow and suffering, toil and tribulation that we gain the education we have come to class for in the school of human experience.

One of the bravest things we will ever do is learn to make wise choices and decisions and then accept responsibility and accountability for those choices. The responsibility must be accepted—good or bad, positive or negative. We must cease blaming everyone else for everything that is negative, difficult, or unfair in our lives. Somehow we must break the bonds of the credit-card mentality that blankets modern society, the mentality that says "get now and pay later." We must always pay in the end no matter how long the payments are put off. If we are responsible, we will pay now rather than waiting for some future pay-off date or life-altering event. Steven R. Covey speaks often of the law of the harvest, and anyone who ever lived on a farm or tried to grow anything knows this law well: We cannot plant at the end of the summer or only feed our stock properly prior to the sale and expect an acceptable harvest. Why can't we learn that happiness and peace will come when we spend our time and energy in goodness and obedience to law and principles right now rather than saving for some future life correction or repentance?

An often told story illustrates this point beautifully.

The story is of a young Indian warrior who made a trek up the sacred mountain to commune with the spirits. As he climbed higher and higher up the mountain the temperature became colder and colder. He wrapped his buckskin tightly around his neck in order to keep the biting cold from chilling his flesh. As he rounded a turn in the trail, there before him was a dying rattlesnake. The snake had not made it to warmer ground soon enough and was unable to crawl with precision, for the cold air made him stiff and groggy. At first the warrior was frightened, until he realized the snake had no strength to strike. As he contemplated what to do to get around the snake the snake spoke to him.

"Please, brave warrior, save my life. Please pick me up. Please help me get warm so that I might make it back down the mountain to my home."

The warrior responded. "If I place you in my shirt next to my skin and you receive warmth and strength you will bite me and I will die."

"No," whispered the snake. "I promise. If you will warm me and take me back down the mountain with you, I will not bite you. I give you my word."

The warrior thought for a few moments and then asked the snake, "Why should I trust you? You are a snake and you will bite me and I will die."

105

"No," responded the snake again. "If you will warm me and give me life I promise that I will be your friend and I will not bite you."

Again, the young warrior boy contemplated and decided to trust the snake. "Surely," he thought, "if I give the snake new life he will be appreciative and spare my life."

The warrior bent down and gently picked up the rattlesnake, placing it securely next to his skin under the protective buckskin. He then proceeded up the mountain to accomplish his mission. After communing with the spirits he began his journey down the mountain. As he descended lower and lower the sun became warmer and warmer, and the chill of the high altitudes was no longer present. As the sun warmed his skin he felt life coming back into the snake. The snake soon said, "Thank you so much, my friend. We are now near my home. Please place me on the ground and I will forever be in your debt."

The warrior carefully reached into his shirt and, speaking kindly to the snake, thanked him for keeping his word and gently placed him in the dirt. Without warning, the snake coiled and struck the young warrior just above the ankle. With the venom burning as it entered the bloodstream, the warrior cried out in pain and disbelief: "I helped you. I saved your life. I believed in you. How could you bite me when I was so good to you?"

The rattlesnake calmly hissed, "You knew what I was when you picked me up!"

Are we like the young warrior? Do we foresee and know, at times, what the result of our choices may be but believe that negative results such as addiction, death, hurting others, or loss of life or limb will never happen to us? The warrior tried to blame the rattlesnake, but the snake put the responsibility right where it belonged. The warrior knew what the snake was when he picked him up. He should never have believed him. He knew he was a poisonous snake.

Do we take the time to contemplate what the results of our choices may be, or do we just act, hoping to have fun or a good time with little or no thought of what follows our behavior? Can happiness, peace, and freedom ultimately result from such disorganized living? We must learn to recognize, by being good, those pitfalls that would destroy inner peace, security, happiness, and freedom. The power to recognize these pitfalls—or these "rattlesnakes"—and know when to run from them is another power that comes from being good.

Chapter Nine

The Power to Run!
The Power to Love!

For some reason, I have been afraid of spiders much of my life. I don't know why, but they have always disgusted me. Of course they fill an important role in the food chain; nevertheless, they're still creepy. As time goes on they are becoming more tolerable to me. Most are harmless and will not hurt anyone, but I still try to shy away from them whenever possible.

One night, while enjoying a blissful sleep, I was awakened by my wife calling my name over and over. "There's something in our bed! It just ran across my arm, and it's big!"

I unwillingly crawled out of bed, turned on the light, pulled back the covers, and in a somewhat irritated voice said: "Are you happy now? See, there's nothing in our bed. You must be having a nightmare. Please get back in bed and quit worrying. There's nothing here but your dreams." After turning off the light and crawling back into bed I attempted to take advantage of the remaining hour before it was time to get up. It didn't last long. Just a few seconds later Melanie stood up on the bed and, in fright, called out again. "Honey, it just ran across my face and it felt hairy!"

This was unbelievable. Again, somewhat put out, I got out of bed, turned the light on again, and pulled back the covers. "Good grief, Melanie, you're having a nightmare!"

We searched the entire bed. No spider. Finally, I grabbed my pillow and, pulling it to the edge of the bed, said, "Let's just go to sleep!" Then I saw it. On the bed where my pillow had rested was a large, brown, hairy spider. It scurried so quickly that it appeared to jump to the top of the pillow, which was still in my hand. Letting go of the pillow as if it were a hot iron, I instantly leaped for the corner of the room. It's embarrassing to admit all this, but I yelled, "Kill it! Kill it!" Melanie began to laugh. "I don't believe it," she said. "My big football-player husband, who thinks he's so tough, is afraid of a jumping spider?" She then went to the kitchen and brought back a quart jar and a plate. (I was still in the corner.) She carefully got the spider into the jar and placed the plate on top as a lid; the spider tried to crawl up the side but kept falling to the bottom. With taunting motions, Melanie kept moving the bottle toward me with out-stretched arms, trying to get a reaction. I stayed in the corner, moving my arms in karate fashion, trying to keep the bottle as far away as possible. We have both had many laughs over that night, but have also learned many lessons from it.

A couple of weeks later Melanie and the children went to Arizona to visit her parents. They were gone for almost two weeks. During that time life was busy and hectic for me, and needless to say, the dishes were not washed or the house cleaned. The night before their return I decided to clean things up. As I cleared the dishes and put them into the sink to be washed, something moved on the counter. From a brief glance it appeared to be rather large, and I thought it ran behind the flour, sugar, and cookie jars.

Instantly, thoughts of the spider returned. Jokingly, I thought this might be the spider's mother coming back for revenge. In my mind I envisioned moving the jars and having a leaping spider lunge for my neck—I guess I'd seen too many movies.

I cleared a pathway to the jars for easy access, wrapped a dishtowel around my hand, and prepared to smash whatever was there. I raised the towel-wrapped hand and with the other hand quickly moved a jar—and a mouse ran out on the counter, frantically looking for an escape route. I tried to smash it with my covered hand but it was too fast. Before anything else could be done the mouse ran to the edge of the counter and leaped onto my T-shirt. I went crazy as it made a screeching sound and tried to get traction while moving up my chest. Trying to knock it away, I flailed my arms wildly, my hands hitting my chest in rapid motion as if I were playing a drum. Finally the mouse fell to the floor and dragged its wounded body under the refrigerator; later that night it was caught with a trap.

The next day as I drove for several hours to Arizona to pick up my family, I marveled at my fears. How could it be that a grown man with children and many responsibilities was afraid of a spider and a mouse? These creatures were basically harmless and were probably more afraid of me than I was of them. There had to be a lesson somewhere. How could phobias be used for something beneficial?

What if each of us, including our children, were just as afraid of self-destructive behaviors as we are of spiders and mice? Why don't we just run from negative, life-altering actions as we do from small, mostly harmless creatures? Some of us, as mentioned, wouldn't get near a "jumping spider" and the thought of a snake, rat, or mouse disgusts many of us. But what happens when life-destroying drugs, relationships, movies, videos, music, or opportunities for criminal activity present themselves? Do we run, or are we afraid of what people will think of us rather than of how our actions will influence our futures?

One of the most significant powers of being good is the confidence and strength that come with a succession of right choices, the strength to avoid activities and entertainment that go contrary to our moral convictions and principles.

111

Before the temptation raises its ugly head we have already spent our energy and time deciding what we will and will not do, and the decision then becomes a predetermined one. When taught in this manner, our children don't have to continually keep making the same difficult decisions over and over. We all have a moral compass to follow which gives us direction.

Tragically, there are those who have chosen and will choose not to run. Some of them, it may be added, have been taught what is right by their parents. We must not lose hope. We must not give up. As long as people have the freedom to choose there will always be those who believe: "It will never happen to me." "I'm different." "I'm more mature for my age." "I can handle it." They simply refuse to accept the reality that to every choice and action there is a consequence, positive or negative. "If you dance you will always have to pay the fiddler." We must learn to run! Being good and staying true to our values and convictions will do more in the short and long run to help us run in times of distraction than just about anything. Again, there is power in being as good as you want to be.

Reading the newspaper or watching the evening TV news allows each of us a small glimpse into the tragedy that follows in the wake of the decision not to run. Daily we hear of young people and adults drinking themselves to death, gang members taking the lives of innocent people, drug deals gone bad, suicide because of the inability to overcome addictions and depression, and abhorrent sexual crimes fueled by the pornographic profiteers who have no other motive than to make money. The actions of youth who are desensitized to the abnormality of behaviors and lifestyles portrayed in some music, television, movies, and videos seems to capture major headlines, not to mention the shattered homes and countless tears they cause by families and parents who feel helpless. These loved ones of those who have chosen not to run stand broken-hearted, wondering where they ever went wrong as they see their children, brothers, sisters, and friends suffer as a result of poor decisions.

Unfortunately, there are those who sink so low because of their inappropriate choices that they never do get out of the self-destructive trap. While speaking at a leadership seminar for high school student leaders, their advisers, and guidance counselors, I had a sobering experience. During the seminar we had been discussing the importance of avoiding behaviors that can have a negative effect in our lives. After the speech several people asked me rather specific questions about some of the issues we had discussed. One question came from a guidance counselor at a local high school. He asked, "Have you been following the murder trial of [let's call him Bill] on the local news?" I indicated that I had because the young man being tried for murder was a former student of one of my teaching colleagues; the young man had called my colleague from jail and asked him to come and talk with him shortly after his arrest. The murder had made headlines in most major papers around the country. As the trial progressed, the local media reported on the story almost every day. All of us standing there in the room knew what the counselor was talking about.

"Well," he continued, "I was his high school guidance counselor. Shortly after his arrest I met with him in jail. We talked for some time about the entire situation. I then asked him a penetrating question.

"Bill, how did someone like you, from a strong and stable family, with a good upbringing, go from being active in school and church to skipping school, forsaking church, to drug addiction, devil worship, and murder? How did your life take such a tragic turn in just three years?"

Bill's unhesitating answer to the counselor surprised even me. I don't know what I expected, but his answer floored me.

"My music," he had said. The counselor continued to quote Bill.

"I wanted to be just like my heroes I was listening to. They sang of death, drugs, violence, sex, and the occult. I wanted to know what it was like."

A local newspaper article (from the Utah *Deseret News,* 1 Nov. 1997, p. A6) and Bill's words, as told to me by the counselor, give us insight in to why Bill's life took the road it did. (All the details cannot be shared because of the graphic nature of the story.) Bill said, "'I'm not making any excuses because there are no excuses. . . . If you say drugs were the turning point, you've got to ask way I did drugs in the first place. You keep going back further and further looking for answers. There is no turning point. It's the whole piece of everything that happens."

The first blemish on the portrait of young Bill's life, ordinary as it seems, came in the first grade, when the rest of the class learned to count to one hundred. "I couldn't do it," he said. "I couldn't get past nineteen. I felt completely humiliated."

Bill said one of his teachers arranged her students in order of intelligence as she perceived it. The brightest sat on the front row. "Whoever was sitting in the last row, right seat, was stupid. And that was me," Bill said. "The problem I had was that I looked like a normal little boy and acted like a normal little boy and played like one . . . so what is wrong with me? Why am I so flawed?"

"Bill suffered from dyslexia, a relatively common reading impairment often associated with genetic defects or brain injuries. He didn't learn about his condition until he reached death row.

"I always felt lesser," he said. "Really, you just want to be like everybody else. Your whole life at that age is going to school."

School only got tougher. He found ways to anesthetize himself. At twelve, according to a history he gave psychologists, he was drinking. At fifteen a group of lifelong friends asked him if he wanted to try marijuana.

"The second I did, wow!" he said. "I had found my niche in life. I finally found what I was good at. I could drink and party and do drugs like nobody else."

The counselor then related how drugs had taken over Bill's life at a very early age; on the night of the murder, Bill and his companion were high and had been listening to heavy-metal music. In need of money, they decided to rob a convenience store. That night during the robbery Bill murdered an innocent woman.

The counselor concluded by asking me to share this story when speaking to young people with the hope that it might help someone. He said Bill had asked him to relate it to as many as would listen so they wouldn't end up as he did. I assured the counselor the story would be shared whenever possible. After thanking him, I walked to my car and drove home with a heavy heart. It was literally sickening to think that a nineteen-year-old life had encountered and caused so much sorrow.

Not long after my discussion with Bill's counselor, Bill was convicted of first-degree murder and sentenced to die for his crime. I will never forget watching the evening news as Bill gave his final plea for mercy before the sentence was read. His hair was cut neatly and he was dressed in a sharp-looking three-piece suit. The tears flowed as he read a written statement. He said he had learned many lessons since the crime and that for the first time in years he could see clearly without his mind being clouded by drugs and alcohol. He wanted his life to be of value to the youth of the country. He expressed his desire to help young people understand the world of drugs, the occult, and heavy-metal and punk rock music. He didn't want the lessons he'd learned to be wasted by killing him. As Bill finished his plea, the news clip then moved to the judge's response and the reading of the decision of the court. As I remember, the judge simply stated, "Your desires are admirable and I agree that you might be able to help other young people. However, your crime is so heinous that you will die for having committed it." What a tragedy! Nineteen years old and sentenced to die.

Perhaps the question should be asked: Will anyone listen to Bill's story and learn? Is there some way that Bill's tragic experience can be used to stop someone from following the same path?

The purpose of sharing Bill's story is not to suggest that everyone who becomes involved in the behaviors he was involved in will become murderers, but it does show what can happen if a person allows him—or herself to avoid running from dangerous situations. The challenges many of us face as a result of poor choices may not be as dramatic as Bill's, but they can still bring sorrow, disappointment and unhappiness that could be avoided.

How then does being good give us the power to run from negative, life-destroying decisions? How do we gain the power and the strength to not be negatively influenced by our peers? Remember "Bill"—he just wanted to fit in, even if it was as the best drug and alcohol user. As parents and adults we must give youth a sense of belonging. Remember, this was one of the major steps in becoming builders rather than destroyers that was discussed in Chapter Five. Everyone needs to belong! Everyone needs friends who will strengthen them, and someone to confide in, even if that friend is a parent, teacher, or other adult in a young person's life. Everyone needs someone to share their dreams, hopes, and visions with, without fear of feeling stupid or rejected. We all have a basic need: we must have significant responsibilities in order to feel we are contributing to a family, community, organization, worthwhile cause, to something that matters. Otherwise we may contribute to unworthy causes. People just want to make a contribution somewhere. They want to belong.

While speaking at a banquet many years ago, I found a small piece of paper stuck in a cupcake. The words on that paper have caused deep reflection. They read, "The entire sum of existence is the magic of being needed by just one person." Doesn't every human being have this desire? Most people want to be someone special. John Dewey stated, "The deepest urge in human nature is the desire to be important. It is a gnawing, unfaltering hunger. People sometimes become invalids in order to win sympathy and to get a feeling of importance. Some authorities declare that people may actually go insane in order to find, in that dreamland of insanity, the feeling of importance that has been denied them in the harsh world of reality." People matter. In order to really love and build them, we must be obedient to true and correct principles. We must run from negative influences that would corrode our foundation of goodness. The power to love and the power to run are directly related, and linked to ones ability to be good.

With this understanding, a significant question must be asked: What if you are the one who feels unloved? What if you are the abused, the downtrodden, the forgotten? What if you are the one sitting on the "stupid row" in the back? What if you are the one who is made fun of or is on the blunt end of every joke? How do you get others to love you? How do you learn to forgive and to love? Again, remember a concept taught in a previous chapter. As you love others first, in most cases, eventually they will love you in return. There will always be those who have become so hard-hearted and self-centered that their love waxes cold. But for most the principle is true—as you love them they will love you.

In the department where I teach, each year at Christmas several service projects are initiated among the students; these generate thousands of dollars. The funds are used to provide Christmas gifts for many families in the area; most are struggling single-parent families who would basically have no Christmas if not for the love and concern of many wonderful young people. One of my colleagues received the following letter from a young man who had been involved in one of the many fund-raisers. To me the letter exemplifies this important principle: many times, when we show love and concern for others, they will love us in return and then desire to give to others.

Dear Miss Rasmus' class,

I am writing this letter and having Miss Rasmus read it to you because I was extremely touched when I found out what your class was doing for this family. The reason why is because when I was nine years old my family was going through an ex-

118

tremely difficult year. My father had to file for
bankruptcy when he lost the two pharmacies that
he managed, my brother had to have surgery on
his knee, shoulder, and ankle from a football injury, my sister Laura had her appendix taken out,
my father had a heart attack and five bypasses
from the stress of losing his stores, my sister Jana
got married, my grandfather died of cancer, and I
broke my leg. After all of these occurrences in
1987, my family was very short of money. My
parents were very afraid and worried what was
going to happen to my family. As Christmas came
upon us, my parents gathered all eight children together and told us that we were not going to have
much of a Christmas that year. We all understood
completely and all felt very low and down.

Christmas Eve came and it was a very
melancholy night. During Christmas dinner
someone came over to our house—we don't
know who, but when we opened the door we
found three garbage bags full of presents for all
of my family. That was a very rare experience,
for it was only one in a few times I have ever
seen tears of joy in my father's eyes. That
Christmas was turned from gloomy to joyous in
a matter of minutes, just by the showing of love
and care for my family, by someone else in our
greatest time of need.

That Christmas was one of the greatest and
fondest Christmases of my life. I was so thankful
for all the love people showed me and my family
that Christmas. I am just thankful for all the will-
ingness and love your class had for this family.

When I was asked to help put Christmas lights
up at people's houses [in order to raise money
for others' gifts], your love and charity struck me
very hard. It struck me so profoundly that I
would like to dedicate my paycheck of Thanksgiving week to your family and cause, for I was
helped and I am sure the family you are helping
is just as thankful. That is why I would appreciate your accepting my check for $170.00 into
your fund. I want to thank you for thinking of
this wonderful and loving idea, for people like
you are what makes a child's Christmas go from
sadness to joy. Thank you again.

Love, [John]

"From sadness to joy." None of us has a perfect life. As expressed in this young man's letter, life is often filled to capacity with challenges and hardship. But as we love others
first, hopefully we can have a small part in turning their lives
from sadness to joy. When part of our personal struggle
comes from feeling unloved or not needed, it would be wise
to allow the magic of loving others to first weave a golden
thread of character into the tapestry of our lives.

The power to run from self-destructive and dangerous
influences is a power that each of us needs in order to find
true happiness, because as we run—from the "spiders" and
"mice" if you will—we find the inner strength to love ourselves, as well as others, even when we feel rejected or
snubbed. This is not always an easy principle to live, but
as with so many other truths in life, it is the difficult skills
we master which bring us the most joy and the greatest
measure of long-lasting peace.

Chapter Ten

Music and Our Lives

O ne of the great responsibilities of parenthood is to help our children learn to make wise and responsible decisions. Helping children learn that there are consequences to every decision, and providing them with tools to make those decisions, enables them to be self-reliant and functional when they leave the security of home. In the next couple of chapters we will explore a very sensitive topic: the idea that music profoundly affects us in many ways and that it can greatly influence the atmosphere in families. We will also cover some ways to help our families in making responsible choices about what they choose to watch and listen to.

How important is music in your life? If you're like most people, you would find it difficult to live without music, in some form or another, on a regular basis; very few lives are not affected profoundly by this magnificent means of communication. Regardless of what we choose to listen to—whether it be rock, jazz, classical, country and western, new wave, punk, heavy metal, reggae, rap, grunge, alternative, speed metal, death rock, devotional, religious, or elevator music—in most instances the music has a noticeable effect on our actions, feelings, thoughts, and spirituality (not to mention hair and clothing styles.) Simply put, we are seriously influenced by our musical and visual diet. I believe we are as much what we listen to and watch as we are what we eat. We become what we think about most of the time, and whatever we choose to fill our minds with influences our behavior. Actions, feelings, and attitudes grow out of our thought patterns.

Volumes have been written about music. Armies have been motivated by it; teenagers camp for days to purchase tickets to hear it; athletic events would often be dull without it; movies and television have come alive because of it; airwaves buzz with it; religious leaders, as well as their followers, sing praises to God through it; and unfortunately, many families have been and are becoming disrupted by it.

I know of few things that can influence human behavior more than the power of music. It is one of the most powerful stimuli known. Like food, music can be enjoyed immensely without any real knowledge of how it was prepared or packaged; perhaps this is why so many people, young and old alike, are involved so deeply and so often in their music. It provides a chance to fantasize, to live dreams through the successes and lives of others in the private and sometimes quiet chambers of our minds. By immersing ourselves in music, it is possible to escape the many pressures and stressful situations created by our modern society.

Music has been one of the most common expressions of man's feelings since the beginning of human history. Man has always sung. Many of the great thinkers of antiquity emphasized the powerful effect of music upon the character of man. Confucius, Plato, Aristotle, and many, many others were convinced that music molded character. Perhaps the old axiom "As in music, so in life" is more a truism than we realize.

For civilized man, music has become an international language. Feelings that words simply cannot express can be effectively communicated by music. Though the words to a song can be translated into many different languages, the music itself communicates to the soul.

Through music, human beings are able to express themselves beyond the limits of the spoken language in both subtlety and power. Music can be used to uplift and enlighten or to carry messages that are negative and destructive. Perhaps we should give more thought to and be more selective about the music we listen to.

It is almost impossible to say that music does not affect us in one way or another. Surveys have shown that the average American teenager listens to more than four hours of music each day (*Newsweek,* 28 October 1985, pg. 46). If this survey continues to be even remotely accurate today, then there are very few teenagers anywhere in the modern world who are not influenced and who do not hear a number of hours of music each day.

Sometime ago while hiking in the mountains with my father, I had an experience that helped me better understand the pervasive and all-encompassing nature of music. We hiked to the top of a rather high knoll. When we reached our destination, we found a comfortable spot under a tall, bushy pine tree to sit and observe our surroundings. A beautiful sight opened to our view as we sat and watched the mountain below us, as well as the vast mountain range surrounding our secluded perch. There were miles and miles of tree-covered hills on all sides of us, with meadows of sagebrush and tall grass spotting each ravine and gully.

There I sat, alone with my dad, exchanging whispered conversation, drinking ice-cold water from a canteen, and eating apples and miniature Hershey chocolate bars. It was wonderful! It was the first time we had been in the mountains for several years and we simply wanted to be together and enjoy the beauty and wonder of nature away from the pressures of our hectic lives.

As the sun fought to make its way over a group of early-morning clouds, we enjoyed each other's company and the bliss of that moment. Then, without warning, the bliss was interrupted as the soft eastern wind brought with it—of all things—the sound of an electric guitar. It became louder and louder with each second. It wasn't long before we spied the source of the piercing rhythms bouncing their way up the mountainside: A would-be hunter in a late- model four-wheel drive pickup, evidently with an outrageous sound system, was enjoying his music at an extremely high volume. When he reached the top of the knoll below us, he stopped the truck, opened the door, and stepped out. I could not believe it! The speakers attached to the door were sending screams of music across the valleys and dells, with little respect for the two men seeking solitude beneath the pine tree. If there had been any wildlife to observe in the immediate area, they were now well on their way to a new and more quiet hiding place.

When the driver of the truck finally turned off his stereo, I turned to my dad and said, "See, Dad, what have I been telling you? Music is everywhere! We can't even get away from it on the tops of the mountains."

Obviously we didn't see any wildlife or receive much solitude, but we both learned something about music. We learned that just about everywhere we go, even to the tops of the mountains, music is all around us.

Think about it. Could you go thirty consecutive days without listening to any type of music whatsoever? Even thinking of it is difficult—some readers may even go through withdrawals while considering the idea. I invite anyone to try it. You will find it almost impossible. Why? Because music is everywhere! Thirty days without music means no shopping at the local supermarket. No visits to the dentist's or doctor's office. No shopping at the mall! You can't even get put on hold on the telephone if you don't want to hear music. No music for thirty days means no live athletic events, no television, no videos or movies, no radio, no concerts, no dances, no parades, no plays, not much of anything; in fact, we wouldn't even be able to attend most schools. It is difficult to visit any high school, college, or university without hearing a myriad of types of music. Thirty days with no music would also mean we would not be able to attend most church meetings, for many religions use music as a form of worship or prayer.

Thirty days without music would be practically impossible. Oh, it might be done with a great deal of work and effort, but for most it would be a very difficult task. After all, what is the first thing many people do when they get up in the morning—especially teenagers? They turn on the radio or CD player. Some even wake up to a clock radio! On many days, the first thing pumped into their systems is music. Is it possible that it could have a profound effect on their actions, feelings, and thoughts?

Not only is it the first thing many people experience in the morning, but oftentimes it is also one of the first things we do when we get into our cars. After starting the engine it is almost a natural reaction to immediately begin pushing buttons or turning knobs until we find the tune we want. Then, a strange human phenomenon occurs: the windows go up, and we begin to have our own concert inside the car. The person driving begins to tap out the rhythm of the tune on the steering wheel, sometimes even singing into a thumb, an imaginary microphone. The person in the passenger seat plays his imaginary drums or piano on the dashboard. Heads begin to bob like large birds during a courting ritual, and facial expressions, along with sincere and serious singing, tell the story of the music being listened to. Some people speed up or slow down or just kind of space out, depending on the kind of music they are digesting.

It is hilarious to pull up beside people like this and watch as they fantasize themselves into the dream world of being a star. Most of the time these stoplight performers have no idea how they are acting until they look over at someone in another car who is watching and being entertained. They immediately realize that they are making fools of themselves, and they flip their heads forward in embarrassment and conclude their concert. However, when some people know they have an audience they intensify their level of performance, to the enjoyment of all who are watching.

If listening to music is the first thing many people do when they get up in the morning and one of the first things they do when they get into a car, what is the last thing many people do when they go to bed at night? Some people can't even sleep without the narcotic of music; yet some claim it has no effect on them. How many parents or brothers or sisters have crept silently into a loved one's room late at night or early in the morning to turn off a radio or CD player that was left on because the room's occupant was unable to sleep without it playing?

With this type of powerful and continuous influence in our lives, would it not be wise to be cautious when choosing the type of music with which we surround ourselves, especially if we consider that some studies have shown that teenagers listen to an estimated 10,500 hours of rock music between the seventh and the twelfth grades? That works out to just about five hundred fewer hours than the time they spend in school over twelve years. Children between the ages of two and twelve watch an average of twenty-five hours of television a week, and most of the programs are accompanied by a musical score (Ibid.) Music is important, and it can be a wonderful, exhilarating form of entertainment. On the other hand, some types of music, with their negative lyrics, rhythms, and beats, can prove to be disruptive to family settings and create a negative atmosphere.

Contention in a home is one of the great tragedies of life. Often music can be a contributing factor to that contention. When someone yells down the hall, "Turn that garbage down," what is the most common reaction of the person being yelled at? Isn't it usually to turn the music up instead? Battle lines are drawn over what is acceptable and what is not. Parents at times become enraged at some popular music, and children sometimes feel that their parents' music is old-fashioned and slow. It can become a contest of wills: each defends his/her position regarding who is right and who is wrong without considering what is right for all involved.

With the rising of tempers it is soon forgotten that just because a person likes the music does not make it appropriate, and just because he or she dislikes it does not make it inappropriate. For this reason we must base our decisions concerning music on true and time-tested principles rather than on personal tastes. For example, we may enjoy the feeling of driving a car off a three-hundred-foot cliff— it's probably a real rush all the way to the bottom. However, when the car hits the ground we're talking major-duty pain. Just because you may enjoy the ride does not mean it is good or healthy, and so it is with music: Just because you enjoy what you are listening to does not mean it will have a positive influence in your life. As with many other areas in our lives, contention over music can be destructive. Contention, in any form, can be devastating to a family. It divides us and keeps us from wanting to build loving relationships.

For me, there is no worse feeling than to be at odds with those I love most. A feeling of darkness prevails, and a sickening nausea and emptiness converge upon me. On the other hand, there is perhaps no greater feeling than to have harmony and peace with loved ones.

I remember a time in my youth when I had a disagreement with my mother. I cried, complained, and even threatened to run away. It was an idle threat, but I threatened to do it nevertheless. After a few minutes of disagreement, I could stand it no longer. I headed for my bedroom with the intention of slamming the door, getting my jacket, and leaving for good. Hurrying down the hallway, I cried out, "You don't love me anymore! You never let me do anything!" The funny thing is, I have no memory of what the disagreement was about.

When my mother heard that I thought she didn't love me, she said something that caused chills to run through my body. She commanded, "Young man, you stop right there!" When my mother said stop, you had better stop! I knew she meant business. She was the type who wouldn't hesitate to chase me down the block, tackle me on the neighbors' lawn, and then bring me home by any means necessary. Seldom, if ever, did she wait for my father to return home before taking care of a problem herself.

I stopped and, with a quivering voice, cried again, "Why should I? You don't love me anymore. You never let me do anything!"

After telling me to stop a second time, she brushed by me and went into her bedroom. She returned shortly with a suitcase in her hand. I stood and watched in utter amazement as she entered my bedroom, pulled out the dresser drawers, and filled the suitcase with many of my clothes. After snapping the suitcase shut, our eyes met. I could see her true sweetness but tried to ignore it. I knew she could sense that I was uncomfortable and did not know how to handle such an abrupt action—after all, I was her sweet, spoiled, baby boy. I had always felt that she thought I was something special, but now I didn't know what to think, and she knew it!

We were still exchanging bold stares when she spoke and nearly broke my heart. "Jackie," she said, handing me the suitcase, "if you think you can find a better mother than me, or one who loves you more than me, go ahead, leave."

My little broken heart was telling me not to leave, but my pride told me I needed to teach her a lesson. I left. Where was I to go? In the early 1960s in our small community the only alternatives were the playgrounds at the school; the apple, peach, pear, or cherry orchards surrounding our home; the irrigation ditch; or the horse trailer parked in the field behind our house. The horse trailer won out; I climbed on the outside wheel well, threw my suitcase in, and climbed in after it.

I remember how terrible it was to be in the trailer. It obviously hadn't been cleaned in years, for it was filthy and the smell was almost stifling. However, I was determined to stay there no matter what and, as I said, teach my parents a big lesson.

It wasn't long before I fell asleep. I didn't wake up until I heard my dog barking and jumping up and down at the side of the trailer. When I came to my senses, I could hear my dad calling my name. I quickly tried to quiet the dog before he gave my hiding place away: however, it was too late. In the middle of one of my quieting attempts, the trailer tipped to one side—the moment of reckoning had come! My dad had climbed up on the wheel well and was peering down at me like death itself.

Up until that time in my life I wasn't sure if prayers were answered, but I prayed without ceasing for deliverance. Almost before my prayers had a chance to get out of the trailer, my dad commanded in his deep and somewhat angry voice, "Young man, get out of the trailer now!" I was petrified, so I pretended to be asleep. He gave the command once more. My pretending continued. He didn't wait to ask a third time: with one motion he reached down with his thick hand and pulled me over the side of the trailer and set me on my feet. My hands immediately went to my backside for protection; however, the expected swat never came. Instead, he placed his strong but loving arm around my shoulders and said, "Oh, son, I'm so glad I found you. Your mother and I have been worried sick. Won't you come home and eat dinner with us?"

I replied with a sigh of relief and thanksgiving, "Uh . . . yeah, I guess I could." We walked arm-in-arm back to the house. As we walked through the door and down the hallway, I could smell the familiar aroma of my mother's cooking. When I reached the end of the hall, I stood at the bottom of the two steps that led into the kitchen. There she stood, her apron smudged with spills, her hair disheveled, her glasses on the end of her nose, and tears in her eyes. She walked to where I was standing, knelt down on the floor, and placed her tender hands on my cheeks. This time, as she looked in my eyes, I melted and my pride ran back to the horse trailer. She cried and said softly, "Oh, Jackie, will you ever forgive me for being such a terrible mother?"

I fell into her arms and muttered through my tears, "You're the best mother in the whole world!"

Looking back in time and comparing the nausea of fighting with the bliss of harmony, my heart aches. Why are we so foolish as to let little insignificant items destroy the beauty of peaceful homes? Why are some young people and their parents willing to let the most sacred and important relationships in their lives—those with their families—be marred or damaged for such minor, temporary things as the cost of a CD that will only be popular for a short time or a video or concert ticket? Music does play an important role in contributing to contentious situations in our daily lives, as well as in our homes.

I know of an individual who had a startling experience while riding on a plane with Mick Jagger, the lead singer for the Rolling Stones. They discussed many items of importance, including contention over music within the family unit. This individual said that Mr. Jagger felt a great need to free up the youth. He felt that the young people ought to be able to do whatever they wanted, in spite of their parents, and that parents were inhibiting them and controlling things, and that parents shouldn't do that. The individual said he was astounded when Mr. Jagger told him that he was thankful that the family, as a entity, was being destroyed.

This supports statements made earlier by Mr. Jagger in an article that appeared in *Newsweek* magazine in 1982. He said, "There's no future in rock 'n' roll. It's only recycled past. ... Basically, rock 'n' roll isn't protest, and never was. ... It promotes interfamilial tension. It used to. Now it can't even do that, because fathers don't ever get outraged with the music. Either they like it, or it sounds similar to what they liked as kids. So rock 'n' roll's gone, that's all gone." Perhaps this is why some artists have moved into areas in their performing which will offend many parents.

What are we to believe when at least one well-known performer is so vocal about the fact that much of his music is written for the specific purpose of causing contention in families? It's frightening. In fact, the lead singer of one group declared that he and the other group members "wanted to be the group parents hate." Why? Because then music would be purchased as an act of rebellion, thus increasing the performers' financial security. Money is the name of the game for music promoters, with little thought given to the effects on the consumer: If a product generates revenue, it is produced.

In no way am I trying to say that all of society's ills can be blamed on rock and roll and that all contemporary music is evil; I'm simply trying to illustrate that music is an important part of our lives, and we can help our children by encouraging them to be selective in their choices. In the next chapter we will learn some significant ways to help anyone, youth or adult, make educated musical and video choices.

Oh, that we could only let the edifying and lifting powers of music fill our minds and souls. William E. Gladstone, the nineteenth-century British prime minister, put it this way: "Music is one of the most forceful instruments for governing the mind and the spirit of man."

Hopefully each of us will be more conscious of the magnificent power of music and also of some of its destructive powers so that we may enjoy music as one of God's greatest gifts. As Henry Wadsworth Longfellow expressed in his poem *Christus*: "Yet music is the prophet's art. Among one of the gifts that God has sent, one of the most magnificent."

Chapter Eleven

Music, Children, and Choices

As a teacher I have long believed the now-popular statement, "If you give a man a fish, he has food for a day. Teach that man to fish, and he has food for the rest of his life." This statement became a part of my life while in graduate school many years ago and has greatly influenced me. It reminds me of a story about a fleet of fishing boats that docked each afternoon for years at the same pier. Each day as they entered the dock, the shiphands would clean their fish and throw the remains into the water. The seagulls in the area would flock each evening to the pier, hoping to find dinner and take part of it back to their young.

For years the seagulls obtained plenty of food; they never had to work for themselves. The fisherman provided everything. As a result, the seagulls never learned to fish. Then one day the fishermen and their ships did not return to the familiar pier but went in search of more fertile waters. As a result, the seagulls missed their evening meal. Days passed, and no ships thus, no fish. Each day brought death to large numbers of birds, and eventually most of the seagulls in the region died. They had been hand-fed for so long they had not learned one of the most basic and simple elements of life: how to feed themselves!

How can we help our children successfully make significant choices in music, media, and all other areas of their lives so they will not become like the birds at the pier? How do we teach them to fish so they have the skills and the tools to not only survive but to thrive when we are no longer a daily part of their lives?

The late Dr. Bruno Bettelheim, who taught at the University of Chicago for years and was an internationally known child psychologist, said, "A teenager has to make judgments based on quality. But he cannot do that by himself. He needs help, and to provide it parents must have good judgment themselves. If they watch [or listen to] trash, how are they going to develop a child's judgment?" (*U.S. News and World Report,* 28 October 1985, p. 55). Often whatever is the most popular entertainment of the time is blamed for everything, but much in the media can be made constructive if parents take an interest.

As parents are we regularly sitting down with our children and, in a calm manner, asking them about their entertainment? Or have we turned their musical and visual education over to the local radio station, movie theater, computer, or video store? Most children are delighted to discover music and movies of genuine merit when their parents help make them available. Bringing great music and videos into the home can be an enriching and exciting experience not only for children, but for parents as well.

What are the criteria we use in helping children choose appropriate entertainment? How do we teach them to "fish," rather than just tell them what to do? Before answering these questions let us consider what a powerful role music and entertainment plays in our actions, feelings, and thoughts.

Some time ago while attending a symphony concert, I had an insightful experience. The performance was marvelous, and the music was uplifting, edifying, and resounding. It left me with a wonderful feeling. However, I almost missed hearing the music because of those sitting near me.

Just to my right was a young man sitting with his mother, totally engrossed in the music. At times he would have to restrain himself from clapping during each number; at other times he was tapping his feet. Then, without any notice or warning, tears rolled down his cheeks as the symphony played songs that touched his heart. I found myself entranced by the effect the music had upon him. Later I noticed an older gentleman sitting two rows in front of me. He was singing the words to himself and conducting the music as if he were in front of the stand, moving his hands in a 4/4 beat and then a 2/4 beat, matching the rhythm of the song being performed.

I could not help but say to myself: "And people say music doesn't have any effect upon the way we act, think, or feel?" It was entertaining and educational not only to watch and listen to the symphony, but to watch the audience as well.

One of the most fascinating phenomena in the world is the manner in which music affects human thought, feeling, action, and spiritual awareness. As I travel, I never cease to be amazed at how hairstyles, dress, speech, attitude, social behavior, recreational choices, and other activities are affected, each in its own way, by the music an individual devotes himself to, and by the heroes and heroines of that particular genre of music.

See for yourself: As you go to the store or to a ballgame, observe how many of the styles you observe had their beginning on a poster or CD cover, in a popular movie, or by a popular musician promoted by radio, video, or music television. Indeed, much of our modern environment is affected by music, visually as well as aurally.

It has been said that music creates atmosphere; atmosphere creates environment, and environment influences behavior. The basic mechanics of the atmosphere/environment/behavior relationship are rhythm or beat, volume, intensity, repetition, and lighting.

Many consider rhythm to be the very heart of music because of its profound effect on the individual. Rhythm, a patterned measure of time, causes the natural tapping of the foot, the fingers, or a pencil as we listen. Small children are interesting to watch because of their total honesty and lack of inhibition. Without having been taught the intricacies of music, they instinctively begin to move in time with whatever music they happen to hear. It is rhythm or beat that causes such actions.

Rhythm is the most physical element of music. Some reseachers believe it is the only element of music that can be felt by the body without the benefit of sound, and research also shows that a mind dulled by drugs can still respond to beat. Other researchers maintain with the ears completely blocked, the body still responds to sound. This is because we "hear" not only with our ears, but also with our bodies.

Some psychologists believe that music influences the digestive, secretory, circulatory, nutritive, and respiratory functions of the body. Musical sounds can be manipulated so as to induce alternating states of tension and relaxation. The melody can affect the larynx involuntarily. As notes on the musical scale go up, there is more tension; down brings more relaxation. It can affect the heart, skeletal muscles, motor nerves, and repeated patterns can cause light hypnosis. Sustained chords can lower blood pressure; crisp, repeated chords raise it. Loud volume stimulates responses of hormone secretion in addition to nervous and muscular tension.

A fascinating study was conducted by Dr. John Diamond and is recorded in his book *Your Body Doesn't Lie.*

Dr. Diamond made an in-depth study of the function of the body as it is affected by music. His discoveries are quite remarkable, but very logical. His major thesis concerning music is that because of the heartbeat and the rhythm of the music, our bodies are profoundly affected. The "da da dah, da da dah" beat, known in poetry as the anapestic beat, is common in many rock records. However, its effect appears to be different when used with music than when used in poetry. "The rock beat appears to be addictive; repeated exposure to it causes one to seek it. It becomes the beat of choice." He goes on to say that our bodies are physically affected and our muscles are weakened by this particular beat. It is almost impossible for the muscle to have full strength while listening to the anapestic beat. On the other hand, many muscles are strengthened with other types of beats and rhythms.

He does mention that not all rock songs have this weakening effect, nor does the music of any particular group necessarily have the effect consistently. His studies found that earlier rock 'n' roll songs did not have the effect that the hard rock music of today does; in fact, by testing more than twenty thousand records of all types of music, he found that the only type of music other than hard rock which caused the muscles to go weak was Haitian voodoo drumming.

According to Dr. Diamond, not only is this particular rock beat addictive, and not only does repeated exposure cause one to seek it, but it throws the entire body into a state of alarm. It causes major changes to occur in children. Their performance in school decreases and hyperactivity and restlessness increase. In fact, the academic records of many schoolchildren improved considerably after they stopped listening to rock music while studying.

In adults, Dr. Diamond found a decreased work output, increased errors, general inefficiency, reduced decision-making capacity on the job, and a nagging feeling that things just weren't right. He goes on to say that the major problem he saw was a loss of energy.

More recently Drs. Frances Rauscher and Gordon Shaw of the University of California, Irvine, have done research that supports some of Dr. Diamond's conclusions. They found that having children take music lessons, encouraging them to enjoy music, and perhaps playing Mozart concertos for them can significantly enhance their abilities to learn. Dr. Rauscher suggests that by giving children music lessons as early as possible, parents may be able to improve "reasoning abilities . . . crucial for such higher brain functions as music, complex mathematics, and chess." (In this study, the researchers advocate that music programs in schools are of such importance that they should never be eliminated.)

Dr. Rauscher indicates that it's not known what type of music works best to improve their intellectual capabilities, but "the more complex, apparently the better." In other words, according to her research children apparently are better off listening to or trying to play Mozart than they would by spending time on rock music with repetitive lyrics and rhythms. While simply having your children listen to music apparently improves their intellectual capacity, actually learning how to read and play music seems to have a much more dramatic effect.

A number of studies have been conducted at universities across the country concerning the effects of music on the physical body. For example, the behavior of unruly and hyperactive children is markedly improved by playing background music. The use of popular children's records resulted in marked improvement in children's behavior. Also, the productivity of hyperactive children in a schoolroom setting is enhanced by the utilization of musical stimulation. It has also been found that unborn children are affected by the music their mother is exposed to. Children who are read to or talked to or have music played to them while in the womb have been found to react to sound and vocal stimuli better than those who have not received such stimulation. They are also found to be soothed much more easily when music is played.

Music has a marked effect on us even while driving in stressful traffic. It has been found that the chance of an accident is reduced when the car radio is on. I know this seems crazy, but institutional studies have shown that music played at peak accident periods has resulted in a lower accident rate because music can offset the effect of nerve-sapping tensions and aggressive driver reactions, which often build up during these stressful time periods. Some music (mood, instrumental, choir, and semiclassical) has even increased the production of nursing mothers' milk by as much as 50 to 150 percent. Does music have an effect on our bodies and our actions? Of course it does.

What about our thoughts and feelings? Are they as affected by the music we listen to as are our actions? The evidence, again, points overwhelmingly to yes. Tolstoy said, "Music makes me forget my real situation. It transports me into a state which is not my own. Under the influence of music I really seem to feel what I do not understand, to have powers which I cannot have." (As quoted in Bob Oliphant, *Music and Its Effects,* typescript, p. 15.)

In the previous chapter we have already discussed the significant influence music has on our everyday lives. Most of us go about our lives giving no real thought to how the music we listen to, the videos we see, or the words we sing affect our minds and feelings. Could we be much more careful about what we let filter through our minds? Remember, we are, or will become, what we think about most of the time.

Napoleon Hill, in his classic book *Think and Grow Rich,* said, "Our brains become magnetized with the dominating thoughts which we hold in our minds. And by means with which no man is familiar, these magnets attract to us the forces, the people, and circumstances of life which harmonize with the nature of our dominating thoughts." They lyrics, the words, the scenes from the videos constantly flowing through our minds cannot help but have an effect on what we think and how we feel.

Remember, we can in reality forget nothing. Every experience, every word becomes a part of our lives and our being. In recent years this idea has been demonstrated by researchers conducting studies during brain surgery. Drs. Penfield and Robers of the Montreal Neurological Institute have literally confirmed that we don't forget anything: It all is stored in our brains. It is just a simple matter of recall, not of remembering or forgetting, but of bringing it back. During brain surgery when they stimulated certain brain cells with an electrode, the patients on whom they were working reported the sensation of reliving scenes from their past. Their recall was so vivid that all details were present, including sounds, colors, and odors. (Denis Waitley, *The Psychology of Winning* [New York: Berkley Books, 1984], p. 95)

Where does music fit in all of this? In addition to being one of the most effective ways we have to learn things, music also has other positive effects. When people become depressed, studies show that they often resist strenuous verbal efforts to cheer them up, but investigators at a leading university found that depressed subjects responded favorably to lively, exciting music, because it affects people on an emotional rather than a rational level.

When a young person becomes angry in the home, what does he or she do? Although this isn't always the case, it has been my experience that many will retreat to their rooms and crank up the music as loud as possible. Why? Because the music harmonizes with the feelings they feel. We usually want to listen to music that agrees with how we want to feel about ourselves, others, or current circumstances. Selecting music that coincides with a person's actual mood is known by psychologists as the "iso-principle." When using the iso-principle for a person who is depressed, downbeat music is matched to the depressed mood. Then, by stages, the music is changed to more upbeat music, thereby altering the mood of the subject. As one investigator pointed out, matching the mood of the music to the mood of the person is necessary because otherwise the subject will reject it; but by degrees we can shift the music and carry the subject's mood into a more tranquil state.

Does this information help somewhat in answering questions as to why so many people today are angry with society, with the world, and with themselves? Take a look at the music they listen to. What videos are they watching? Are they filled with violence, anger, or both? Have we found violence to be the cure to all of society's woes? If society is constantly viewing graphic violence as entertainment, should it be surprising when violence shatters the dreams and lives of its youngest and brightest?

Many, many studies have been conducted on the powerful influence of music on human beings, plants, and animals; they are far too numerous to mention in this book.

However, if we're going to teach our children how to choose appropriately, we must understand the impact music can have on the entire human organism. With something so persuasive on the actions, feelings, and thoughts of our children, should we not spend time helping them understand the importance of choosing wisely?

When it comes to music and other forms of media, have we as parents become like the birds at the pier? Do we yearn for someone who is more familiar with who is popular in the music industry and who is not to give us a specific list of musicians to avoid? We and our children can learn to choose for ourselves, without a current pop music chart, if we learn to apply correct principles.

What would happen if I included here a list of what I thought was appropriate and inappropriate music? How long would the list be current? By the time this book is published, the list will be outdated. In addition, you would simply have my own opinion, which means little because it may not be entirely correct.

What are the major principles in choosing? Two simple questions can help solve this complex problem. 1. Do your music or your videos promote a positive, constructive lifestyle that builds individuals and families? 2. Or does your entertainment promote or encourage a lifestyle contrary to your religious or family values? When asking questions in order to evaluate the positive or negative affect of entertainment, four areas need to be considered.

1. *Lyrics.*

What if the music is wonderful and exhilarating, but the words or lyrics are negative? Often when I speak on this subject, parents will say, "Well, I can't understand a single word they say anyway. How do they listen to that stuff?" The younger people generally respond with, "I don't listen to the words. I just like the rhythm and the beat."

Studies have revealed that it makes little difference to most listeners whether they understand the words or even pay attention to them, but for many, the minute words are put together with music, they're cemented into the memory. It's amazing how we often sing or hum tunes with words that we would never dream of speaking. It's also amazing how many students have a difficult time memorizing facts and information, but they know every word of every song in the Top 40. I love the simple phrase, "A song will outlive all sermons in the memory."

Have you ever stopped to consider why the characters on *Sesame Street* almost always use music to teach? A young mind simply can more easily assimilate and remember information when it is set to a catchy rhythm and beat. Big Bird, Cookie Monster, and the Count always use music: "One, two, three, four, A is for agua!. . ." Even Barney the Dinosaur uses music to say, "I love you, you love me. . . ." You'll never forget it, even if you hate it! Think about how you learned your ABCs. Was it through music? Of course, and the tune was "Twinkle, Twinkle, Little Star!"

While thumbing through a local sales brochure advertising a childrens musical cassette program, I noticed that it cited some interesting figures. "Children remember 10 percent heard, 40 percent story, 60 percent visual aids, and 90 percent that is taught by music. Teach your children through music." If these figures are accurate, it is obvious that words accompanied by music play a far greater role in our lives than most of us have ever imagined.

Some time ago I was driving down the freeway with my radio playing when a song by the Beatles came on. In an instant my mind rushed back to the late sixties, and I began to daydream while singing and pondering. I caught hold of some pleasant memories from my past and remembered some activities I had participated in while listening to that song so many years before. As I sang, I never even missed a comma. I remembered every single word. It had been at least ten or twelve years since I had heard that song, but the lyrics were vivid in my memory.

It is easy to say that the words are not important or that they're not the major part of a song. However, when they are constantly in our minds it is hard to throw out the teaching that as a man "thinketh in his heart, so is he" (Proverbs 23:7). In fact, could it be that we are as much what we listen to or watch as we are what we eat? The only difference is that instead of the material coming into our bodies by way of the mouth, it enters through our eyes and ears. It becomes a part of us! Becoming what we think about most of the time is not a new concept to the advertising industry. Very few commercials on television or radio are not accompanied by catchy jingles or memorable musical scores.

For years advertisers wanted nothing to do with the flamboyance of the rock industry. However, it didn't take long for them to change their minds when dollars were involved. Most rock stars are much more business oriented now than in times past, and money is the name of the game. For monetary purposes many advertisers have used rock 'n' roll to sell their products. Oftentimes they use the music from songs of the past in their jingles so that the consumer will immediately recognize it.

Simply put, the lyrics do make a difference and are programmed into our minds whether we like it or not. With the advent of music videos, lyrics have become even more important in the selling of products. Think for just a moment: If Saturday morning advertisers can sell a box of cereal in thirty seconds, can music promoters sell us a lifestyle or an idea in a three minute video? Lyrics put to music, combined with well-designed images, become a powerful communication and teaching tool. For example, very few of us purposefully memorize the words to daily television or radio commercials, but with repetition they often become a part of us, programmed into our thought patterns by their connection with unforgettable tunes. It is always interesting to ask adults to fill in the blanks of a commercial that hasn't been on TV since the early 1970s. They almost always know the ad though they haven't thought about it for years. "Winston tastes good like a _____ should." Did you get it? What if I use another old commercial such as: "You deserve a _____ today, so get up and _____ _____ to _____" Did you get that one? Chances are you probably did. But do you know any of the details of any commercial selling inusrance to those over age sixty-five? Most people can remember very few details because those commercials generally don't have music playing in the background. Why? Because advertisers don't want the young consumer to buy insurance until they are older!

If the lyrics, then, are in harmony with that which will encourage positive behaviors and support family values, then enjoy it! If they do not, it might be a good idea to eliminate them from our musical or visual diets.

2. *Music.*

The next major question when choosing music or other forms of entertainment addresses the music itself. What if the words are positive but the music itself affects you in a negative way? Suppose it makes you feel depressed, angry, or violent. Is it harmless? Or can we listen to anything we want and not be influenced one way or the other?

Can music in and of itself, regardless of lyrical content, have an influence on the way we act, think, and feel? Research shows that music will generally cause in a person the attitudes and emotions that the composer intended. It can excite. It can mellow. It can relax. It can agitate. It can lift spiritually. It can depress. It has many other influences.

To illustrate this point, let us again refer to television and movies. Even before movies had sound there was always an organ or a piano to create mood and to communicate feeling to the audience. What would a movie be like without music? How would we ever know during a scary film that someone was hiding in the closet? How would we know when to feel romantic, when to be nervous, when to be excited, when to cheer? If music were eliminated from movies, moviegoers might seek out new forms of entertainment, for obviously films would simply be too boring to maintain our attention.

One of my favorite examples of music's significant effect during a movie is in the soundtrack to the classic motion picture *Jaws.* If there had been no music during the opening scene, the movie would have lost much of its impact because viewers would have had no idea what was going on. However, with the music, the entire story line becomes clear.

The movie begins with a young girl swimming near the beach. As she swims, she suddenly begins to make jerking motions, and she gets a look of terror on her face; without music, the viewer wouldn't know if this young woman was having a violent internal reaction to something she had eaten, or hit her feet on the jagged coral below. By adding music to the scene, the viewer begins biting his fingernails, wincing with fear, curling up in his seat, or screaming, "Get out! Get out!" Even without seeing it the audience knows that a great white shark is about to attack the girl. The music is a cue: the crowd moans with terror and vows never again to go swimming in the ocean.

The producer, performer, and arranger all have certain objectives they wish to achieve, whether it be to stimulate, depress, agitate, inspire, or uplift. However, we must remember that the name of the game in the music industry, or any media industry for that matter, is to make money. It is a business, and that which is going to increase revenues, good or bad, is that which is going to be sold and produced. It has always been thus. It is often easy to adopt a low standard of moral values, because it sells.

Again, music will generally do what it is written to do. Therefore, as parents, we must use wisdom in our own listening habits if we are going to help our children use wisdom in theirs. It would be well for all of us to take a little time to thoughtfully evaluate and be careful about the musical content of the entertainment we choose.

3. *CD and tape covers;*
names of musical groups.

Often young people argue, "But I don't listen to the covers." Obviously not and the covers may have nothing to do with the music inside; it may simply be a technique to promote sales. However, if the CD or cassette-tape covers are promoting drug abuse, violence, destruction, etc., or are covered with gross illustrations, my advice to parents would be to sit down with your child and ask well-thought-out questions. Reason together calmly about the appropriateness of having such material in your home. Some may feel this is unnecessary, but remember, by asking rather than telling, we are teaching. Young people generally appreciate being heard, and they enjoy knowing that their ideas and feelings matter and have value. Ask if they feel that you as their parent would approve of the cover or the name of the group who produced the music. By taking such an approach, we may help young people learn to make appropriate decisions without conflict.

4. *Music videos.*

Does pairing a captivating musical score with a video or movie make the program more powerful or add impact to its message? The answer is obvious! Turn on MTV when young people are present and you can be assured that most other activities will cease and soon the program will have a mesmerized audience drinking deeply from its pictures.

There is something about "seeing" the music which is captivating. Today's listeners spend countless hours viewing what past generations only listened to. With visual images being broadcast simultaneously with audio, the motives of the composer and performer are brought home with force and fervor; nothing, is left to the imagination of the listener. The intent of the song is acted out before our eyes in vivid detail and unforgettable fashion. After watching the video once or twice, the images are planted firmly in our minds and can be recalled quickly and in detail with the slightest stimulus. This medium is really nothing new. News reporters have used the visual technique to strengthen their stories since the inception of the movie theater and television.

I vividly remember going to the moviehouse in my hometown and watching a newsreel before every major movie. Everything from war to horseracing was broadcast, because few people in those days had the luxury of television. Believe it or not, I still remember the content of some of those flickering black-and-white newscasts.

Many years ago Dan Rather, anchorman for the *CBS Evening News,* made a great case for why newspaper readers should also watch TV newscasts: "If you read a good newspaper every day you're going to know most, if not all, of what's on the evening news and probably a lot more, but you won't have seen it. I think there's a difference between reading about the war and seeing some of it." (*TV Show Biz Magazine,* 15 January 1984, p. 41.)

As far back as 1985, social workers were concerned about what young people were viewing on television. They were almost unanimous in citing the influence of the popular media—television, rock music, videos, movies—as increasing the trend toward precocious sexuality. One survey showed that in the course of a year the average viewer saw more than nine thousand scenes of suggested sexual intercourse or innuendo on primetime TV. (*Time,* Dec. 9 1985, p. 81.) In the many years since, have these forms of media that were of such concern in the eighties become even more of a concern?

It is disconcerting to think that with such a barrage of sexuality, the message being broadcast is that to be sophisticated we have to be sexually hip. One author states that we don't even buy toothpaste to clean our teeth anymore; we buy it to be sexually attractive or to make sure we have fresh-smelling breath when we have an encounter with someone of the opposite sex.

Can this barrage of sexually explicit material and violence fail to have a profound effect upon the rising generation? United States Senator Robert Byrd made this observation: "If we in this nation continue to sow the images of murder, violence, drug abuse . . . perversion, pornography, and aberration before the eyes of millions. . . year after year and day after day, we should not be surprised if the foundations of our society rot away as if from leprosy." (As quoted in Michael Medved, *Hollywood vs. America* [New York: *Harper Perennial,* 1992], p. 94.)

Victor B. Cline, a clinical psychologist, professor at the University of Utah, and nationally regarded expert on pornography's influence on society, wrote a thought-provoking article titled "Obscenity—How It Affects Us, How We Deal With It." In this article the problem of "seeing" what we are listening to is brought masterfully into focus. He states:

> The outside world truly has entered into our homes--into the family room, the kitchen, and the bedroom. The seriousness of the problem has prompted this examination of a sensitive and distasteful subject. The media have a great potential to teach, inspire, inform, and entertain, but they may also corrupt, degrade, and pervert. They have the power to influence profoundly for good or evil all aspects of our values and feelings, as well as our behavior. We are affected by what we choose to expose ourselves to.
>
> For example, I have a letter from a fourteen-year-old girl telling of the death of her ten-year-old brother by hanging. With naive innocence, he had imitated the scene of a mock hanging he had witnessed in an evening television movie. He thought he could escape death as the actor in the movie had. He didn't. As a clinical psychologist, I see examples almost daily of gracious and good people (all ages, both sexes) of exemplary upbringing who have become addicted to viewing violence. Many have also cultivated an appetite for voyueristically viewing stimulating, sexually explicit scenes of multiple adulteries, rape, or the seduction of innocents—all in living color and accompanied by a memorable musical score. Evil is presented as attractive and good. Destructive behaviors are marketed as exciting and rewarding. Often humor is used to make pornography, rape,

151

or the loss of innocence entertaining and palatable. But what starts out as a spectator sport introduces into one's brain a vast library of antisocial fantasies. These have the potential, much research suggests, of eventually being acted out—to the destruction of the individual and others around him.

I have found that four things typically happen to some people who become immersed in erotic or pornographic material. First, they become addicted. They get hooked on it and come back for more and more.

Second, their desire for it escalates. They soon need rougher and more explicit material to get the same kicks and excitement.

Third, they become desensitized to the abnormality of the behavior portrayed. In time, they accept and embrace what at first had shocked and offended them.

Fourth, eventually there is a tendency and temptation to act out what they have witnessed. Appetite has been whetted and conscience anesthetized. . . . Those who witness this porno-violence in commercial cinema, on cable television, or on a rented videocassette--and who allow their children to view it--in my judgment do great injury to themselves--and their children. This exposure creates false images and feelings about men and women and sexuality and raises the possibility that the viewer may be conditioned into practicing sexual deviancy. For, as much evidence has suggested, all sexual deviations are *learned,* not inherited.

Would it not be wise for us to fill our lives and minds with the good that exists in this magnificent teaching tool of music videos and movies? Can we not teach our children to be unafraid as they strive to be "as good as they want to be?" The words of Charles Dickens's classic novel *A Tale of Two Cities* ring in our ears: "It was the best of times, it was the worst of times." We live during an era when more is available for our good and comfort than at any other time in the earth's history. However, there is also much material available at the touch of a button or the click of the remote control which can truly be damaging to us and our families. Hopefully, we will have the courage to be good and choose wisely.

A caution: as we educate ourselves and our children on this sensitive subject, it is important to remember that we must lead the way. Child-development experts suggest that parents must take charge. We should be bold but not overbearing. As we teach, it is important to be filled with love and allow our children to choose for themselves. They may choose contrary to what we think is best for them; nevertheless, we should not cease teaching. We cannot be afraid of our children or fear that they might get angry and run away.

President Dwight D. Eisenhower understood this principle: To illustrate it, in a cabinet meeting he would lay a long piece of string on the table. He would pick up one end of the string and try to push it forward, and it would always become entangled. Then he would pull the string, and it would follow freely.

Somehow, if we can gently lead, if we can pull rather than push our children along--teaching by example, love, and patience--perhaps many will follow.

What will happen in our homes when posters that we as parents don't approve of go up on bedroom walls, when styles shift to extreme clothing and hairstyles, when school grades drop and the sweet nature of our child turns irritable? How will we handle such a situation? Here is where I believe we need to take charge, but we must do it in an appropriate way. Hopefully, no parent or guardian would be unwise enough to go into a young person's room and destroy tapes or CDs, or tear down everything on the wall without consulting with the child first. Can we not reason together? Can we not begin to ask questions as to why certain drastic changes in behavior are taking place? If we, as parents, can strive to create a climate in our homes where young people can feel a sense of belonging and feel that they will be heard, it may be possible to difuse potential explosive situations.

Some experts suggest that some dramatic behavioral changes are signals that adults should notice, for they may indicate that entertainment is threatening emotional health. Darlyne Pettinicchio, co-founder of Back in Control Training Center in Fullerton, California, has suggested that music is the number-one indicator of emotional problems. "The troubled kids will be totally absorbed in either heavy metal or punk music," she said. Then a rebellious stage sets in; some even become physically violent and very aggressive, responding to their parents with the "you can't tell me what to do" attitude. Sometimes hairstyles change drastically, and some children may begin to wear dark clothing. Pettinicchio and other experts suggest that enforcing rules for school attendance and household chores is vital, and a ban on certain types of music may be necessary. She cautions that the teenager may get upset, but you as the parent must give clear, direct commands and signals. We must be extremely wise and intelligent in how we go about this process.

Dr. Bruno Bettelheim has suggested that if a child is addicted to a certain kind of music or to a certain musical group, it means there is a gap in the child's life that he or she is trying to fill.

"Many teenagers turn up their music full blast to blast other thoughts out of their heads," he said. "It is a way of getting away from troubling feelings or to fill a void. It's similar to an addiction to drugs. People become addicted not because drugs are around but because of emptiness. If everything in a young person's life is in order, then the media will have very little influence." (*U.S. News and World Report,* 28 October 1985, p. 55.)

The best advice I have ever heard on handling the subject comes from the analogy of a young child picking up a sharp object. Sometimes a foolish adult will grab for it, frightened for the safety of the child, and instinctively the child may grip it more tightly and perhaps injure him- or herself or the parent as he or she pulls away. The wise parent will instead offer some equally appealing but harmless object in exchange so that the child will let go willingly and without tears.

Helping others change requires persuasion, gentleness, and kindness. It is best to provide constructive and interesting alternatives. We should keep in mind that "to tell is to preach, to ask is to teach."

Good luck in teaching your children how to "fish" that they might have food for a lifetime. May you have great success in helping your children succeed as they learn how to make wise choices in their entertainment and other areas of their lives.

Chapter Twelve

Working and Laughing as Families

The Memorial Day holiday is a tender time of year for many people. My family visits two or three cemeteries on that day to honor our dead. One year my wife, her family, and I visited a cemetery where many of my mother-in-law's relatives are buried. The countless flowers of varying colors and arrangements decorated the cemetery lawn. The sun was hot and penetrating. People were everywhere: some were clipping grass from around headstones, others were trying to force flowers to stand upright in small cans or bottles of water. Some simply stood with solemn faces, reading inscriptions and wandering in their minds to happier times. Their faces revealed memories of a time when their loved ones still lived and emptiness and loneliness were distant. It was educational, yet it was also sad to watch and wonder about their many different lives.

As we stood by family gravesites, I listened intently as my mother-in-law told stories about each of the individuals whom we had come to visit and remember. Though the sun continued to beat upon us relentlessly, its rays somehow seemed to be reflected and diverted as the stories of our heritage became more important than our physical comfort. We laughed and cried as we talked and listened. It was good to have been there.

Before long the blazing sun took its toll. We loaded up the trunk of the car with empty flower buckets and boxes and made our way to the cemetery gate. Our plan was to drive to a nearby park and have a picnic. As we carefully tried to avoid people and cars on the narrow one-way roads, we saw a man, perhaps twenty-five to thirty-five years of age, kneeling on his hands and knees as he talked to a grave. At first we thought he was injured and was calling for help, so we stopped the car to look and rolled down the window to listen. He was certainly injured, but not physically: he appeared to be emotionally devastated. We talked for a moment about whether we should get out of the car and render assistance, but our questions were quickly answered. He didn't need us, he needed to let out his pain in solitude. As we watched he went from kneeling to a completely prone position atop the grave. He spread his arms from side to side as if to embrace the buried loved one. With his head turned to one side and his cheek pressing against the grass, his cries and sobbings became audible. This man was beyond grief at the loss of whoever was laid to rest in the grave. The weeping and wailing were more than any of us could take. Our tears flowed freely; we each experienced a lump in our throats which prevented us from speaking. We each felt that we were invading a sacred moment. Quietly, we rolled up our windows and slowly drove to the park in silence.

Since that experience I have thought back many times upon the sobbing and the sorrow of this bereaved man. I have learned that for many, most joys are family joys and most sorrows are family sorrows. Our families and marriages are our primary concerns in this life, and it is okay to weep when loved ones suffer and die. All of us will suffer. All of us will die. Hopefully, all of us will live together in love so that when separation comes, whether it be through death or other circumstances, we are left with few sad or embarrassing memories. Life is hard, and it is a great deal of work, but amidst all the trials, heartache, and work there is much to be enjoyed, especially with our families and loved ones.

Regardless of the type of family you come from (or even if you have no immediate family), much of our time is taken up with family joys or family sorrows. You have probably heard the saying, "The family that prays together, stays together," and in most cases this is probably true. But to stay close, create pleasant memories, and remain friends, it could also be said, "The family that works together, laughs together, reads together, stands together, loves together, plays together, stays together!" Solid stable families take work! Life is work! If we have not helped our children learn to work, we have in some degree failed them. I can think of few things more difficult to achieve and yet few more rewarding than working and laughing beside my children and other family members.

There are so many families in crisis today that many wonder if it is worth the work, pain, rejection, and time to help the family be as good as they want to be. What's wrong with being good in our families? What's wrong with being a team player and trying to help the entire family succeed? Again, if you have a traditional family, a single-parent family, or if you are a family of one or two, it's okay to be as good as you can possibly be! Happiness in any family of any structure or size is most likely to be achieved when the familial relationship is founded upon those principles of goodness discussed in this book. Again, it is okay to follow such good, time-tested principles as faith, prayer, repentance, forgiveness, respect, love, compassion, work, and wholesome recreational activities. Regardless of your family's religious background or lack of religious beliefs, can it hurt a family to build their foundation around such principles as mourning for those that mourn, trying to eliminate the type of pride that says, "You are nothing, and I am everything," being merciful, pure in heart, or being peacemakers? How can a family, regardless of size or structure, fail if each member is committed to the Golden Rule of "Whatsoever that men should do to you, do ye even so to them?"

It seems like fairly common-sense information. Sure, it takes work, but as we have discussed, this business of life is work! Somehow, when we help our children internalize this concept, we will have made major strides toward helping them succeed in any area of their lives. I once read a wonderful passage that illustrates my point beautifully.

There seems to be a superstition among many thousands of our young [men and women] who hold hands and smooch in the drive-ins that marriage is a cottage surrounded by perpetual hollyhocks to which a perpetually young and handsome husband comes home to a perpetually young and beautiful wife. When the hollyhocks wither and boredom and bills appear the divorce courts are jammed. . . . Anyone who imagines that bliss [in marriage] is normal is going to waste a lot of time running around shouting that he has been robbed.

[The fact is] most putts don't drop. Most beef is tough. Most children grow up to be just people. Most successful marriages require a high degree of mutual toleration. Most jobs are more often dull than otherwise. . . .Life is like an old-time rail journey-delays, sidetracks, smoke, dust, cinders, and jolts, interspersed only occasionally by beautiful vistas and thrilling bursts of speed.

The trick is to thank the Lord for letting you have the ride. ("Big Rock Candy Mountains," *Deseret News,* 12 June 1973, A4.)

Marriage and family life are often a test of mutual tolerance at times, but we can be happy amidst adversity. One of my wife's friends made a funny statement that is something of a truism: "Most of the stress in my life can be traced to one of two sources; I either married it or gave birth to it!"

When a person understands these principles and incorporates them into his/her life, anything can be withstood, even the hard lessons. If any reader has not experienced the hard lessons of life, just live a little longer! Each new day has a way of bringing plenty of hard lessons on its own, without any coaxing. The human dramas being acted out in all cultures, races, and economic levels are magnificent teachers. For example, it has been my privilege to teach with a man for a number of years who goes home each day, several times a day, to care for his invalid wife. His love, compassion, and commitment have not only been a strength to many, but have taught me lessons that years of college could not teach. He has become one of the lighthouses on the shore not only for his family, but for his students and fellow teachers as well. With permission I share a personal piece he wrote about his beloved companion of thirty-four-plus years.

My Love

Still, now over thirty-four years later I can tell you the exact spot where I first met her, there in the driveway on a warm May afternoon. When I saw her, I thought, what a beautiful woman.

After a number of dates, one soft summer evening I mustered enough courage to take her in my arms and kiss her for the first time. As I floated on the clouds to my home I thought I knew all about love, and it was great.

Later as we continued to date, one night when everyone was asleep, I knelt down in front of her chair and asked her to marry me. She asked if I was kidding. I said not. When she said yes I knew I was in love forever.

Months later we were married at an altar. She looked as much like an angel as I hope to see in this life. I said "I do" willingly. We gratefully included God in this special relationship.

One night she anxiously informed me it was time to go to the hospital unless I wanted to be a doctor. Later, I walked into the room and saw her tired, but glowing with that precious little life in her arms. I knew that our relationship had changed forever. I was blessed to witness that divine scene seven more times.

During the years we've been married, many of those years I've been a leader in our church. I've watched this valiant woman with one, two, three, then a whole row of little children, taking care of them all alone. I realize that my love has grown with the lessons of sacrifice and love that I've learned from her.

I've known her to load all of the children in the station wagon and take them twenty miles to shop three different stores just to save a little money. She would then bring it all home, unload it, put it away, then fix dinner and smile lovingly when I would come home and ask what she had done that day.

She has taken a wounded child's head in her hands and administered peace and comfort while others rushed about in a panic. She was so kind and understanding even in times of crisis.

To see her counsel with her children was a revelation. She studied, read, and pondered all she could learn on how to be the best wife and mother possible. Then she went out and applied those principles under the direction of God to the benefit of her little flock. They were bound to her and her to them.

I watched her happily read to her children, telling them sacred stories, singing them songs. I came to realize her love was pure.

Nineteen years ago she was diagnosed with multiple sclerosis. She has waged a courageous battle against the effects of the disease. I've watched her struggle out of bed early in the morning to fix breakfast for her family and tend to their needs.

Now as she sits in her wheelchair and needs me to help her do so many things, I now have an important opportunity to serve and support her. I get to do so many services for her. What I enjoy are the personal things that she trusts only me to do.

I see the frustration and fear in her eyes, and the need to be assured, comforted, and held in my arms. Oh, how much joy I feel to be able to serve this intimate companion of mine. Common everyday chores become a labor of love for me just as they have been for her all of these years. I still learn about our love in ways I did not anticipate years ago.

Years ago I thought I knew what love was. Now I find that each day brings a new revelation. Love is made from much stronger fabric than I thought years ago. It is not just the physical attraction that is so glamorized in the popular media of the day. There are so many ways to experience and express the deepening feelings of love that two people feel for each other as they grow together through the marriage covenants that they make with each other and God. I have told my sweetheart, I am yours, you are mine, and we are God's.

My dear friend is experiencing plenty of struggle and trial without going in search of it. For nineteen years now he has taken care of his sweetheart. On that night in May when he fell in love, there was no way of knowing how the final years of their marriage would turn out. They have both now become refined and dignified through the fires and the crucibles of human experience. They live each day as if it were their last, because it may be. They have learned to take advantage of every moment. They know what love is. They have laughed, cried, served, and worked together. In the face of a great trial they have still been able to raise a happy, successful family.

How are you doing in navigating the stormy waters of life? Are you able to keep your head above water or to stay afloat long enough to teach your children how to succeed when life is unfair, trying, and difficult? If you feel you are just barely staying on top, please don't quit trying. As you keep moving forward and strive to apply correct principles and values, everything will eventually, with time, either fall into place or fall out of our lives.

I know my parents thought they were not making much headway with me in their efforts to teach and train and help me be successful. As you look at your children, do you sometimes feel the same way? Don't forget; things are not always as they seem in our hours of struggle and darkness. Time and patience, unfamiliar words in a fast-paced society, have a way of smoothing out our lives, just as the occasional weeding of a flower bed or garden allows growth and blossoming.

When I was a fourteen-year-old, my father taught me a very difficult but important lesson about life and work. He taught me to have integrity, to be impeccably honest, and to love people regardless of their circumstances. The lesson came when we were asked to help hoe six rows of beets at a local farm. The work had to be finished as soon as possible so that the beets would not be wasted, and many people from the community rallied to help hoe the six long rows of beets. It was enjoyable work until the rain started to fall relentlessly. Everyone ran for cover. After about half an hour, it was evident that the rain would not stop any time soon; car by car the members of the community, including the leaders, all left—except, of course, big Jack and little Jack. We sat and waited and waited. Finally my dad said, "Grab your hoe, son."

"What?" I cried.

He said, "Grab your hoe!" His voice was serious. He then said: "We told the man we would hoe six rows of beets. There are only about three finished. Let's go."

We got out of the truck and walked back to the beets through the mud and rain. I was furious! I kicked mud at him and complained the entire time; I don't know how he put up with me. All I know is that it didn't stop raining and we didn't stop hoeing until it was too dark to see. I was not a happy camper! It took years for me to learn the lesson, but it finally sank in. My dad had given his word and that was more important than staying dry or listening to a whining fourteen-year-old. My dad knew how to work and he knew about integrity, and he tried to teach me. As I said, it took years for me to learn what he was trying to teach. But I did learn.

It is easy to feel that our teachings as parents are falling on deaf ears, but should we ever stop teaching? There is a saying in the teaching profession; "You can only peddle fresh fish." Are we keeping our teachings and our families alive and fresh by laughing together, working together, trying new things together, going new places together, setting goals, learning about finances together, rather than just beating the same constant drum of "pick up your clothes, clean your room, do your homework, cut your hair, don't lean back on your chair, grow up, quit whining?" Are our children being "peddled fresh fish?" Do we take walks together, ride bicycles, go on vacations, listen, and talk together? In short, do we do the things we enjoy doing together?

As we constantly strive to peddle fresh fish by being together and building our relationships, it then becomes easier to verbally express our love and affection even if it is difficult. Break the barriers. Go for it. Don't be like the man lying prone on top of the grave trying to talk to his departed loved one. Tell them now. Be with them now. Share with them now before the time of parting arrives.

Just remember, building successful families, children, and individual lives takes time, patience, and unrelenting work. If it were easy there would be no opportunity for growth and progress; perhaps that is why so many today do not desire to have a family and to raise children. If we shy away from family relationships and responsibilities because of the work, pain, and risks involved, there will be no solutions to the world's problems, for whenever God wants to change anything of significance, he sends a new baby into the world.

As we take on the role of training and teaching these little ones as they grow and struggle in a harsh, unforgiving world, we cannot tire of doing our best and trying to be as good as we want to be.

Chapter Thirteen

Not Losing Hope

At 7 p.m. on the evening of October 20, 1968, a few thousand spectators remained in the Mexico City Olympic stadium. It was cool and dark as the last of the marathon runners were carried off in exhaustion to first-aid stations. More than an hour earlier, Mamo Wolde of Ethiopia—looking as fresh as when he started the race—powerfully moved toward the finish line, the winner of the grueling 26-mile, 385-yard event. His teammate, the legendary Abebe Bikila, winner of the two previous Olympic marathons in Rome and Tokyo, had been forced to retire from the race after 10 miles because of a broken bone in his leg.

As the remaining spectators prepared to leave, those sitting near the marathon gates suddenly were aroused by the sound of sirens going off and policemen blowing whistles. Confused, the spectators looked toward the gate. There, entering the stadium, came a lone figure wearing the colors of Tanzania. His name was John Stephen Akhwari. He was the last man to finish the marathon. His leg was bloodied and bandaged, and he grimaced with each step. He had severely injured his knee in a fall. He painfully hobbled around the 400-meter track.

The spectators who remained rose and applauded the courage of this man as if they were receiving the winner. Akhwari painfully finished the run and crossed the finish line. Then he slowly walked off the field without turning to the cheering crowd. Asked why he had not quit, since his task was so painful and he had no chance of winning a medal, he said: "My country did not send me 7,000 miles away to start the race. They sent me 7,000 miles to finish it." (*Parade*, 21 April 1991, p. 6.)

We are not on earth only to begin life but to finish it. As each of us approaches the finish line, we may be bloody, bandaged, and grimacing with every step. Our race with mortality may have taken its toll, but as we move forward, doing the best we can do, if we can but endure—not quit, but finish with dignity—our life and our suffering will not have been a waste but instead a grand success. There is no need to take a Kevorkian exit: What the world needs is finishers!

Not losing hope. Not getting discouraged. Not giving up. These are some of the challenges we all face as we strive to be good and stay true to our value system. Being good is challenging because we are imperfect and we live in an imperfect world. It is easy to lose hope if we concentrate only on those imperfections. In the King James Bible the Greek word translated as "perfect" can also be translated as "complete, finished, fully developed." Alternate translations from the Hebrew for "perfect" are "complete, whole, having integrity." Is any one of us complete, finished, whole, fully developed? The answer, of course, is absolutely not! And in order to be complete, whole, finished, etc., we would certainly need more than one lifetime, so being perfect doesn't necessarily mean being completely without flaw. We must be careful as we seek to be good and improve our lives that we do not become discouraged and lose hope. Again, it is a lifetime pursuit and very often involves growth and change that is slow, almost imperceptible. We often read or hear of people whose lives changed dramatically, in an instant—or so it seems. Such astonishing examples of the power to change can lift and reach even those deepest in despair.

But we must be cautious as we discuss these remarkable examples, for though they are real and powerful, it has been my experience that they are more often the exception than the rule. For all those who change in an instant, there are hundreds and thousands of people who find the process of change and being good much more subtle, much more imperceptible. Day by day, little by little, they are better and better, trying to do good, little realizing they are achieving their goal: being good. They live quiet lives of goodness, service, and commitment, and they generally have no idea that they are influencing others. Remember, most change and doing good does not involve sensational or dramatic reversals, but rather is a step-by-step, steady, and consistent movement toward living moral principles. Hopefully we will not be so concerned with the speed with which we travel but the direction in which we are traveling. That direction, if it is leading toward goodness, is the all-important factor.

It is always helpful to look to others' examples of goodness. The following story is about a family who did not lose hope in the face of life's most tragic and trying circumstance. Instead, they continued to do good and live life to the fullest.

> We'd just cut the watermelons at a Sunday School picnic and I was laughing at the kids' antics—"playing" the sweet pink slices like harmonicas, making big green grins with the rind, spitting the seeds.

"You seem so happy," said a woman next to me. "How do you do it after . . . all that's happened to you?" Again and again, people ask me that question-people who know that Louis and I had three children who died of Cooley's anemia. First Rosemarie, then Marylou, then George.

How can I be happy? Well. . . .

Marylou was born in 1955. She was our second child, two years younger than our healthy daughter, Ann. At first I thought Marylou's pale skin merely meant she took after me. Although Louis and I are both of Mediterranean descent, he's the one with the olive complexion. Marylou's pediatrician wasn't so sure. "She seems anemic," he said, and he had her tested. Afterward, the doctor called Louis and me in for a consultation.

"I'm sorry," he said, "but your baby has thalassemia major." In this rare genetic disorder, commonly known as Cooley's anemia after the doctor who discovered it, the bone marrow does not manufacture the proper type of adult hemoglobin, the blood protein that carries oxygen to body tissues.

"It mainly affects people of Mediterranean heritage," the doctor told us. Wanting a second opinion, we took Marylou to the Children's Blood Foundation Clinic at the New York Hospital Cornell Medical Center. There, a doctor confirmed the diagnosis. He also said that Marylou would have to come back to the clinic every two weeks for a blood transfusion.

From then on, I drove my daughter into New York City from West Paterson, New Jersey, regularly. After a few months, she got used to it. And she had company; nineteen other children were being treated there for the same illness.

Louis and I wanted more children, but now we wondered.

"Don't worry," our own doctor assured us. "This very rarely happens twice in a family."

Rosemarie was born in 1959. She looked fine— bright blue eyes and fine brown hair like Marylou's. But something was wrong. One day she'd seem perfectly normal, the next her head would be sweating. The pattern had been the same with Marylou. Finally, when she was six months old, doctors confirmed that Rosemarie would also need transfusions.

So now I was driving two little girls into the city. It was easy to see how much they depended on the transfusions. As the time for a treatment neared they would tire easily and become irritable. But after their hospital visit, grueling as it was, they seemed happy again. Meanwhile, Louis and I tried to hide our anguish by giving our three daughters a normal life, with music lessons, games, and family outings.

In 1961 our son, George, was born. We had yearned for a boy, and had been assured our chances of having another child with the same affliction were virtually nil. But from the first moment I held my little boy, I knew. Soon I was taking George into New York along with two-year-old Rosemarie and six-year-old Marylou.

Even so, Louis and I were grateful for our four lovely children. As the years passed, the transfusions became part of our lives, and we went on hoping that a medical breakthrough would make them unnecessary.

Then came our shocking discovery. One morning at the hospital one of the other mothers handed me a newspaper clipping headlined: BAFFLING, FATAL BLOOD DISORDER. It was about children coming to that very clinic. *"Many die before they are 20,"* the article said.

I couldn't believe it. I asked our doctor, "Is it true?"

"Yes," he sighed. "I'm afraid it is." There was no known medical help to prevent my children's death at a young age.

For years Louis and I lived in a daze. His reaction was to say little and concentrate on his work as a garment designer. Mine was to cry whenever I was alone or with the other mothers at the clinic.

We couldn't bring ourselves to discuss it with our children, though I knew that from talking with the other patients, they understood the seriousness of their condition. Then came one of those small but significant moments that changes the way you see things.

I'd walked into nine-year-old Rosemarie's room one evening and found her making a jeweled butterfly pin. "How beautiful," I said, as I watched her carefully set a rhinestone. She was already selling her work at craft shows.

"Thanks, Mom," she murmured. "I'm going to earn all I can toward college."

College?

I cleared my throat. "Uh. . .what are you planning to study, honey?'"

She looked up, eyes shining. "Nursing, Mom. I want to be like those nice women at the hospital."

She turned back to her work, and I walked slowly out of the room, trying to take it all in. Rosemarie was *not* thinking about death; she was focusing on life.

At Thanksgiving, one of her teachers phoned me. The students had been asked to write about what they were most thankful for. "I thought you'd like to hear Rosemarie's answer," the teacher said. Her voice trembled as she read, "I thank God for my good health."

Good health? How could she write that? Then I remembered the other children Rosemarie saw in the hospital, the ones with amputations or cancer. Rosemarie could walk, go to school, skip rope.Rosemarie had filled our home with Scripture plaques that she made. In her own room she'd hung one that read: *This is the day which the Lord has made; let us rejoice and be glad in it* (Psalms 118:24).

I saw then that our house was not a house of shadows and sorrow; our children filled it with cheer. Marylou's piano music rang through the rooms. Rosemarie busily crafted jewelry and plaques. Little George had an extensive rock collection; he was already talking about becoming a geologist. Slowly, I began to see that my children, all of them, were rejoicing in life.

On July 4, 1969, Rosemarie, now ten, was in the hospital with a cardiac problem, a side effect of Cooley's. "You seem better, honey," I said to her that night as I kissed her good-bye. "I'll be back in the morning with Daddy."

Just after I got home, the telephone rang. Rosemarie was gone. "Peacefully," the hospital said.

We mourned. My faith was profoundly shaken. I fought battles with God, kicking and screaming, trying to find answers. Then, little by little, I came to a true understanding and discovered life *can* go on.

Marylou and George had known their lives would be short, but with Rosemarie gone they were forced to face that fact head-on. Marylou, four years older than Rosemarie, began carefully tending her sister's grave. I knew she must be contemplating her own death. And yet she took up life with new vitality. She began making the honor roll in high school and was very popular. And she made a suggestion that gave new direction to our lives.

Louis and I had taken the children on a vacation in the Pennsylvania mountains. Soon afterward, Marylou returned from her hospital visit in a thoughtful mood. "Mom," she said, "when I told the kids at the clinic about the Poconos, most of them said they'd never been to a place like that. Could we take them with us next time?"

"Of course," I said, hugging her.

Right away I organized a volunteer group to take the clinic children on trips. Through bake sales and candy sales, we raised enough for an excursion to the Poconos. How wonderful it was to see the children laughing, having a good time away from the sting of needles, transfusion and spinal taps.

In 1973 Marylou graduated from high school as a member of the National Honor Society. She had undergone surgery for removal of her spleen, so had worked extra hard for this honor. In the fall, she entered William Paterson College as a fine-arts major. Soon she made the dean's list. She worked part-time in a TV repair shop, and her civic activities collecting for charity, and other volunteer work put her in touch with almost everyone in town.

The following year she volunteered for an experimental drug treatment for Cooley's anemia. She had to be hospitalized for three weeks. "But if it helps other kids, it's worth it," she said.

Marylou was nineteen that Christmas of 1974. In January, our Christmas tree was still up. For some reason I just couldn't take it down.

On January 20, a heavy snow kept us all at home. Marylou practiced her piano in the morning, but she was exhausted. "I think I'll rest for a while," she said as she went to bed. Later I brought her some lunch.

"Oh, this soup is so *good!*" she exclaimed. Then the light went out of her eyes, and she fell back on her pillow.

Marylou's funeral was one of the largest ever in West Paterson. The mayor and the entire city council were there. In the words of the Cooley's volunteer group who honored her, she had "lived and understood life better in her nineteen years than most of us could possibly hope to if we lived to be a hundred."

Later, as a cold February rain battered our living room window, I sat thinking about this radiant daughter. On the wall were three plaques Rosemarie had made. *I will never leave thee, nor forsake thee* (Hebrews 13:5). *Casting all your care upon him; for he careth for you* (1 Peter 5:7). *Do not be anxious about tomorrow* (Matthew 6:34). The words wavered in my vision, then cleared. I got up immediately and began preparing dinner for my family.

Our oldest daughter, Ann, was busy with her career. George, a typical teenager, kept our house lively. His friends came and went and the telephone rang constantly. He dated and had an after school job at a restaurant. After graduating from high school, George went on to William Paterson College. He continued working, and the summer he was nineteen he bought a Chevrolet Monza sports car, shiny black with fire-engine-red trim. It was a young man's dream. He kept it carefully garaged and in showroom shape.

That's why, one night in September 1980, I knew something was wrong. George came home from a date, and after he went to bed I noticed that his Monza was pulled into the garage at a careless angle. A few days later he told me, "Mom, I just can't make it anymore. I'm so tired."

That night he said, "I know I'm going, Mom." He looked at me. "Promise me you won't cry? You know where I'll be."

"No, Georgie, I won't cry."

My son smiled, shook his head, and lay back, eyes closed. Then he took a deep breath and was gone.

Rosemarie.

Marylou.

George.

And so, again and again, people ask, "How can you be happy after all that's happened?"

I'll tell you how.

My children understood that life is a holy gift. They loved each day they were given, and their enjoyment and gratitude were like sunlight, warming and brightening our time together. In the face of early death, they embraced life. If they loved life so much—honoring it, reaching out to soothe their stricken friends, using their days creatively—am I to love life less?

No! I will not dishonor God or my children with gloom and self-pity. I will embrace life as they did. I shall rejoice and be glad in it. ("Am I to Love Life Less?," *Guidepost Magazine* [Feb. 1985.])

They did not lose hope! They were finishers! Just because life had been cruel, they did not drop out of the race. They had learned the lesson that hopefully every human being will learn, that as we struggle through life, progressing bit by bit, we learn a little here and a little there. Often we learn the same lessons over and over and over. The Louis and Mary Manachi family had learned that life is sometimes harsh, mean, and unfair. The reality of being human is that there is suffering. There is pain. There is sorrow. But the joy of rejoicing in life and not losing hope is every bit equal to the sorrow, suffering, and pain. In fact, we could not know such deep and abiding joy and happiness if life did not teach us so much about sorrow. It is the suffering that allows us to recognize the joy if we do not lose hope and quit. Remember, "My country did not send me 7,000 miles to start the race. They sent me 7,000 miles to finish it."

Chapter Fourteen

Seize the Day

I n May 1970 something happened in my teenage life that taught me a valuable lesson. The lesson has been my teacher many times since then and caused me to realize at an early age the value of living every day as if it were my last. Much innocence was lost that day as I came face to face with the need to know if the values and beliefs I had been taught all my life were true.

My older brother is a car dealer; he was in the car business when I reached the magical age of sixteen and could start driving. He purchased a 1962 white Cadillac convertible with power *everything* for my sister and me. It was supposed to be shared but I managed to take ownership from the beginning. We called it the "White Stallion." It was so long and spacious, we felt invincible. We would jump into it without opening the doors and the girls we tried to impress thought we were pretty cool.

One afternoon in May my friend Taylor Manning and I drove the "White Stallion" up a local canyon to the hometown ski resort. We wanted to drive up the canyon with the top down, just for fun. As three o'clock approached we headed back down the canyon so I would not be late for my job as a cook at Kentucky Fried Chicken. When we came out of the mouth of the canyon, we decided to take a different way home. That little decision would change forever the way I look at life.

As we came out of the canyon we were traveling approximately seventy miles per hour (that was the speed limit in those days). The traffic coming the other way was thick, but we paid little attention to it as we glided effortlessly down the highway.

It wasn't long before we noticed a group of boys standing at the roadside. We found out later that they were a Little League baseball team on their way home from a practice. They stood waiting for a break in the traffic so they could cross the road.

We slowed down a little and watched them closely. There was a brief break in the traffic in the oncoming lane; without looking in our direction, two of the boys bolted into the street, right in front of us.

It all happened in an instant. I slammed my foot on the brakes and made some quick judgments. I concluded in a split second that if I continued moving straight, I would hit the two ten-year-olds; if I veered to the right, I would hit several of the boys. The only escape from tragedy was to the left, into the lane of oncoming traffic. The decision made, I steered to the left, but at the same time, the two boys heard the screaming of the tires on the pavement and they looked up. One stopped and jumped back. The other jumped forward. The front end missed him, but the car plunged off the road into a weed-filled patch of field, tipped onto the passenger-side door, and skidded through the field into a ditch. Miraculously, the car didn't roll and crush us. We had turned 180 degrees, coming to a full stop facing the direction from which we had come. The dust settled, and we realized the Cadillac was a total loss. We were mad! "Let's go get them!" one of us said.

We jumped from the car to find an unexpected horror. We thought we had missed both boys, but we hadn't. The boy who had jumped forward had been hit by our back bumper as we screeched past him, knocking him about 150 feet down the road. When Taylor and I reached him it was an ugly scene. He had a compound fracture in one leg that was bleeding profusely. His head had evidently hit the large fin of the car just above the taillight, and the impact had caused a massive head wound from his ear across his forehead to his temple, ripping his scalp away from the skull. His skin and clothes were torn off on one side of his mangled body as he skidded across the asphalt. I quickly put a tourniquet on his leg with my belt and put his scalp back in place, then covered his head with my shirt trying to stop the bleeding.

Shock started to set in, but there was little time to notice. At that moment only one thought came to mind. Pray! So I did.

People came from all around to help us, and we were able to stop the boy's bleeding. As we waited for the ambulance, some of the boy's friends, caught up in the emotion of the moment, yelled, "You killed Michael! You killed Michael! You crazy drunken driver. You killed Michael!" I'll never forget those screams as long as I live. They pierced me to the core. Had I killed him? Only time would tell. But for the moment, the screams of little boys rang loudly in my ears. "You killed him! You crazy drunken driver!"

What if I *had* been drinking? What if I had been using drugs? My life would have been dashed to pieces before it even had a chance to begin.

The highway patrolman arrived and took over first aid on the boy. Then the ambulance came and rushed Michael to a local hospital.

Other ambulances soon arrived. They had come to assist the people in a car that had wrecked trying to avoid hitting us. A car filled with a troop of Cub Scouts, coming from the other direction, had driven off the highway to avoid a head-on collision with our car, and many of the boys were hurt severely. It was a nightmare!

As Taylor and I walked to the patrol car with the officer, he insensitively said, "Boys, I sure hope we don't find any drugs or alcohol in the car or in your bloodstreams. That boy probably will not make it."

I sobbed through my tears, "Sir, I don't do drugs! I don't drink! I haven't had anything!" My sobs fell on deaf ears.

As we walked toward the car, my eyes caught sight of a baseball glove and a pair of baseball shoes lying in the road: Michael had been hit so hard that the impact had knocked him right out of his shoes. They were still tied in little bows, lying on the pavement in the spot where his feet had left them. A sick feeling swept over me. "I killed him!" I said to myself, continuing to weep.

Taylor and I went through all the tests, which proved we had not been drinking or doing drugs. It was embarrassing—people driving slowly by, gazing at two sixteen-year-olds being tested by the officers.

Reflecting upon it now, there was no way to have known at eight o'clock that morning that two ten-year-old boys would dart in front of my car later in the afternoon. What if we had been partying before leaving for home? What if Taylor and I had just tried drinking once, and that once was that day in May? No one knows what the future holds. No one knows when the zero hour will arrive. We must live each day as if it were our last or as if it were the last for those we love.

We finally made it to the hospital emergency room to see if Michael was going to recover. As we walked in we saw a tall, distinguished-looking man with his arms around a crying woman. The highway patrol officer introduced us to the couple, Michael's parents. I fell into the big man's arms and cried for him to forgive me. He told me that the accident had been explained to him. He understood that it wasn't my fault and that I had done the only thing that could have been done. He assured me there would be no lawsuit. He assured me that despite Michael's life-threatening injuries he felt confident that his son would be fine and that there was no need for me to worry.

Michael did live. Many days in the following months found me at the hospital visiting him after he had undergone several hours of surgery to repair his broken little body. It took time for him to heal, but today, many years later, you can hardly tell he experienced such trauma.

My life, as was mentioned, was forever altered. I learned that spring day, at a tender age, how precious and fragile life really is for each individual. I learned that one simple decision can alter an entire life and future. I learned how the kindness of one good man like Michael's father can influence, for good, a young boy to want to be compassionate when others make mistakes. I learned that no one can ever say that their life is insignificant and that it matters not how they choose to live. It does matter! It matters for good or for bad. Our lives are not our own. Oh, I know we are individuals and have our independence, but everything we do affects someone else's life.

Each of us has only one life! Obviously we all know that, but the way some of us behave, it appears we believe we are cats with eight or nine lives. At times, we give no thought to the morrow. We live on the edge, giving little thought to the fact that at any instant we may lay our bodies down and depart this life. We eat, we drink, we're merry, not realizing that not only can we die in an instant but our loved ones and friends can die or be taken from us at any time. As John Lennon once wrote, "Life is very short and there's no time for fussing and fighting, my friend." How dare we live our lives without taking advantage of each and every day! We

185

must seize the day! We must live and love each day as if it were our last. This obviously is nothing new, but it is the essence of being good and doing good. We should never wait until tomorrow to make things right. There may not be a tomorrow! Can we not, today, be as good as we want to be? As one of the great teachers in my life taught: "Today, mend a quarrel. Seek out a forgotten friend. Dismiss suspicion and replace it with trust. Write a letter. Give a soft answer. Encourage youth. Manifest your loyalty in word and deed. Keep a promise. Forgo a grudge. Forgive an enemy. Apologize. Try to understand. Examine your demands on others. Think first of someone else. Be kind. Be gentle. Laugh a little more. Express your gratitude. Welcome a stranger. Gladden the heart of a child. Take pleasure in the beauty and wonder of the earth. Speak your love and then speak it again."

How we live today does make a difference. By being good and living by our moral compass we can destroy a whole lot of wickedness in our world. We can change and improve today. We can keep moving forward not drinking, drugging, and partying, but living, loving, and learning. We can save cities. Being good is okay. We can be warriors of light. We can finish. We can be complete. We can be whole. Let us replace our fear with faith. Faith in a happy and bright future. Faith in the right and the good in people and the world. Can we accomplish by being good what King Arthur tried to accomplish in Camelot: "Might for right. Right for right. Justice for all." Can we leave our children and grandchildren a legacy? Can we leave them with stories that they can tell and retell which will teach them and those they teach to be as good as they want to be? Can we help them carry on a legacy of goodness?

On the morning of the great battle after the peace and happiness of Camelot had been destroyed because of lying, deceit, and dissension, King Arthur found a young boy who wanted to join the battle. Armed with nothing but a small bow and a quiver of arrows—he told King Arthur that he had stowed away on a ship in order to come to Camelot and become a knight of the Round Table. The boy's name was Thomas of Warick.

Arthur asked Thomas why he had come to the battle. Thomas replied, "I intend to be a knight."

"A knight?" Arthur questioned.

"Yes, my lord, of the Round Table."

Arthur then asked the boy several difficult questions about where he had learned about becoming a knight. The boy sheepishly confessed that he had never seen a knight until he had stowed away. "I only know of them from the stories people tell."

Arthur then asked, "From the stories people tell, you wish to become a knight?"

"Yes, my lord. I know everything about them. Might for right. Right for right. Justice for all," the boy answered.

Arthur then began to remember and recall the glory of Camelot. He took his sword Excalibur and he knighted Sir Thomas of Warick. He commanded Thomas to run behind enemy lines and go home and live in order to tell people about the glory of Camelot and what had been tried and achieved.

Arthur's servant, Pelinor, reminded Arthur that he must lead his men to battle. Arthur's reply to Pelinor is the last message that I would leave with you, the reader, about being good. He took the boy by the shoulders and cried back to Pelinor, "I have won my battle, Peli. And here is my victory." (It was just one good boy, who wanted to fulfill the commandment of his king to tell others of what can happen when people want to be good). Arthur cried out to Pelinor, "What we did will be remembered. Now, run Sir Thomas behind the lines!"

Pelinor then asked, "Who was that?"

Arthur's response is classic. "One of what we all are, Peli. Less than a drop in the great blue motion of the sunlit sea. But it seems that some of the drops sparkle, Peli! Some of them do sparkle!" He then cried out to the boy—hoping the boy would carry on the dream of the goodness of Camelot—with the same lines that I would use to implore each reader to carry on the desire and the message to be good. "Run boy! Run boy! Run! Oh, run, my boy!" As we run some of us will sparkle. Yes, we will sparkle!

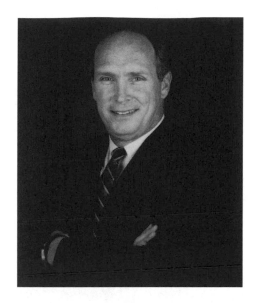

JACK R. CHRISTIANSON attended Dixie College on a football scholarship where he was named All-Conference quarterback. He transferred to Weber State University where he also played quarterback on the football team and graduated cum laude with a B.A. degree in English and Physical Education. While at Weber he was awarded the Outstanding Student in the College of Health, Physical Education and Recreation, as well as the Outstanding Student in the College of Education. He later received a master's degree From Brigham Young University in Educational Administration.

He has worked with young people for many years in different capacities. He has coached football and baseball on the high school level and football on the college level. For over twenty years Jack has been teaching high school and college students. He has been involved with student leadership and been an advisor to many leadership groups. Jack has been involved in administrative roles, serving as a principal twice. He has taught literally thousands of students, affecting their lives in a positive way.

As a highly sought after speaker, Jack has lectured all across the United States and Canada to youth as well as adults. He is the author of several books and numerous talk tapes. He is heavily involved in community and church service and enjoys the out-of-doors; especially his passion for raising dogs.

Jack and his wife Melanie reside in Orem, Utah. They are the parents of four daughters.

ALTI Publishing is dedicated to publishing books which benefit society, families, and individuals. Existing topics include giving, seniors, teens, grandparents, and the environment.

We seek additional book concepts which will help the human condition and assist worthy causes. If you have an idea for a great book, we would like to hear from you.

Tailor-made, special edition books are available for printing in the name of corporations or nonprofit organizations.

Additional Books from ALTI Publishing

From Grandma With Love: *A Legacy of Values*
by Toni Thomas

Drawing upon the collective wisdom and experience of grand-mothers across the country, these real-life experiences will warm your heart, remind you of your life, and inspire your young people to live character based lives. You will love these stories.

Your purchase will help at-risk children because 30% of all sales will be donated by ALTI Publishing to a joint program of the National Head Start Association, National Association of Foster Grandparent Program Directors, and the National Association of Retired and Senior Volunteer Program Directors.

This beautiful, illustrated, hardcover book won The Family Channel Seal of Quality and was a Literary Guild Book Club selection.

Hardcover, 160 pgs., 10" x 7", illustrations, $18.00. ISBN 1-883051-13-4

Volunteering:
101 Ways You Can Improve the World and Your Life
By Douglas M. Lawson, Ph.D.

Discover the joy of volunteering and how to get more from your service. A delightful guide answering all your questions. Ideal for both existing volunteers and beginners wanting to learn.

Softcover, 144 pgs., 5 ½" x 8 ½", $7.95. ISBN 1-883051-17-7

More Give To Live: *How Giving Can Change Your Life*
by Douglas M. Lawson, Ph.D.

You will delight in this revised and expanded version of the award-winning first edition. Learn the joy of giving and how you can enrich your life—quickly and easily. This book also makes a great gift. Americans lead the way in giving to help others—and here is confirmation of the personal benefits; some will surprise you!

Softcover, 304 pgs., 6" x 9", $16.95, ISBN 1-883051-22-3
Hardcover, 304 pgs., 6" x 9", $24.00, ISBN 1-883051-20-7

Additional Books from ALTI Publishing

What's Age Got to Do With It?

Secrets to Aging in Extraordinary Ways by Kelly Ferrin

THIS BOOK WILL BENEFIT YOU!

- Feel young at any age
- Discover a zest for ageless living
- Learn secrets of aging well
- Change your image of aging

If we really belied age was just a number, think how differently we would live our lives. The majority of older adults today are healthy, happy, and believe these are among the best years of their lives. Here are secrets of not letting age get in the way of living.

No matter how old you are, *What's Age Got to Do With It?* is for you. 70% of difficulties typically affecting older people are lifestyle related. Only 30% are genetic in origin. Lifestyle can make a difference! These amazing stories of 103 persons between the age of 67 and 122 will change the way you view your life. Everyone can benefit.

Softcover, 354 pgs., 6" x 9", $14.95. ISBN 1-883051-21-5

"The Message" (video)

by Academy Award winning director, Robert Amram.

A unique and inspiring film of man's connection with nature and the importance of caring for the environment. A poetic and masterful video filmed in the Pacific Northwest.

Digital and stereo, 8 minutes, $8.95

Additional books are available at your local bookstore,

on the internet at amazon.com, or order directly from us.

To order *call 1-800-284-8537*

or write to address below

ALTI Publishing, 15708 Pomerado Rd, Ste. 209, Poway, CA 92064

Fax: (619) 485-9878   E-mail: whilbig@altipublishing.com

Quantity Discounts Available